Thunder Road

originally titled Newfie or Bust

BY
BERNIE HOWGATE

This book is dedicated to
Stan and Denise Steel,
my eye in the hurricane of life

The Travelling Man
Enterprises

Thunder Road
Second Edition

WRITTEN
Bernie Howgate

EDITED
Wendy Reger

MAPS AND ILLUSTRATIONS
Bernie Howgate and Wendy Reger

PHOTOGRAPHS
Bernie Howgate

COVER DESIGN
David Aubrey Berger

PUBLISHED
The Travelling Man Enterprises
67 Centre Street
Schomberg, ON, L0G 1T0
CANADA

First Edition 1998
Second Edition 2018
Printed in Canada

ISBN-0-9694419-2-4

COPYRIGHT @ BERNIE HOWGATE

Tales of a Travelling Man
Based on an eight year round the world cycling trip.
ISBN-0-9694419-0-8

Journey Through labrador
Based on an eight month snow shoe and sea kayacking trip up the isolated labrador coast. .
ISBN-0-9694419-1-6

Lazy Days in Summer
Based on a 4500 km sea kayacking trip from the Great Lakes to Goose Bay Labrador through the St. Lawrence Seaway.
ISBN-0-9694419-4-0

Around the Rock in a Bad Mood
Based on a 3000 km sea kayacking trip around the rugged Newfoundland coastline.
The weather was brutal but the hospitality fantastic
ISBN-0-9694419-3-2

Zen and the Art of Paddling
Based on a 3000 km sea kayacking trip up the Inside Passage to Alaska and beyond.
ISBN-978-0-9694419-5-3

Contact for book purchase
email; berniehowgate@hotmail.com
home page; www.berniehowgate.com

Note:
Bernie Howgate has sold over 60 000 books door to door. These books can not be bought through book stores. Only at the door or by email.

CONTENTS

1. Pay Back Time...page 1
2. No Pain No Gain...5
3. Little Big Man..33
4. Bernie the Bike Man..55
5. Endless Horizons...59
6. Mosquito Country..77
7. Have you ever seen Paris?...................................89
8. Summer at Last...98
9. All good things come to an end.........................108
10. The long green tunnel..111
11. Lake Superior...127
12. Welcome to the real world.................................138
13. La Belle Province...148
14. Humour and Unemployment............................161
15. Five lazy days in Summer.................................173
16. Ocean surf and salted air..................................176
17. The Rock..190
18. God's Country..203
19. The Finish Line..209

MAPS

British Columbia..6
Alberta..34
Saskatchewan...60
Manitoba...90
Northern Ontario..112
Northern Ontario..139
Quebec & New Brunswick................................149
Nova Scotia & Prince Edward Island...............177
Newfoundland...191

Chapter 1
Pay Back Time

Outside the thunder rolled. From my bedroom window the sky was a psychedelic hell hole of jet black, royal blues and shades of red. It was 6:00 a.m. Five hours ago, I was nursing an alcoholic glow. My nerves were shot. I had been downing beers like there was no tomorrow, emptying change into a midnight juke-box and trying my darndest to enter the world of happy endings. Five months before I'd made a promise.Now it was pay back time.

"Hey, Bernie it's arrived."

"What's arrived?"

"The rickshaw stupid. Man, it's bloody amazing. Never seen anything like it."

I was in shock. I'd actually pulled it off. All those letters and phones calls. All those months of embassy red tape. I'd beaten all the odds and got an authentic Pakistani rickshaw and free, to boot. For a moment, I forgot about the phone call. I was flip flopping through time, piecing together events that led me here.I'm not your stereotypical go-getter.I don't create waves, carry banners or stick my neck above the crowd. In fact, I'm no different than your average Joe - that is, except for one small tick.

Ticks,I've been told, are mutant genes. A flu-like bug that gets passed on from one generation to the next. Mine is a fine mixture of Gaelic romance and British tenacity. My tick is the fertile soil that germi-nates ideas like wild flowers. They grow totally out of control. I catch large doses of tunnel vision. Reason flies out of the window,and so it was with the rickshaw. From the start, cycling across Canada never entered my head. I wanted a rickshaw only for display purposes. I had a children's art exhibition coming up. I needed a calling card to attract custom and a bicycle rickshaw fitted the bill.

Since 1988, I had worked steadily through the circuit of Ontario's Boards of Education.I had done the rounds of lecture-cum-entertainer from Elementary to Collegiate. I had billed myself as BERNIE THE BIKE MAN, telling stories and showing slides about a round-the-word bicycle trip I had taken in the mid '80s. Since then, I had visited hundreds of schools, talked to thousands of school children and artwork was the natural offshoot of these visits, so it came as no surprise that most of this artwork related to bicycles. My bike had kept me sane and healthy and opened doors of hospitality at every turn. Now it was front and centre in my talks.Bike ownership, as any parent will tell you, is a pre-teen's first taste of independence. Well, I took it one step further. I made them universal. It didn't make any difference what classroom topic I chose to talk about, or what continent I took them through. I never lost a single student as long as bicycles were in the picture. Whether I flirted with a North American high-tech muscle bike, or took them on a journey through Africa down bumpy roads on a single speed clungster, the show's outcome was never in doubt, but throughout it all, one picture stood out. A Pakistani Rickshaw I took for one ride in the city of Lahore.I lost count of how many times I revisited the back streets of Northern Pakistan with this one slide.It became my signature. The centre piece of my slide shows. For the uninitiated, a rickshaw is a unique blend of picture scene paint work, flashing chrome, mirrors, bells and tassels hanging every where.'Steroid on wheels', I used to call them. They pulled the viewer into a different world. Turned them onto brightness and colour and in the process buried their Third World perceptions of dark, dingy and poverty-stricken.

"Who would like to come to school on this?" A click of a switch and a life-sized rickshaw appears on the screen. "Wow! Neat-o!". Hands shoot up, mouths drop open and two hundred youthful eyes light up like saucers in the sun. After all this, how could I resist the temptation to own one?

In those days Multiculturalism was the flavor of the month, and Toronto's 'Bike Week' was just around the corner. It was a unique opportunity to kill two birds with one stone. Bikes and culture, the media would lap it up. I started by drafting out a letter to the Pakistani Embassy in Ottawa,

Dear Sir,

I would like you to donate...bla...bla...bla...bring our countries closer together...bla...bla...bla...

Then, I pulled in every IOU I could think of, from the Mayor of Toronto to the Explorers Club of Canada. The only thing that was missing was the all-important HOOK. It would be a one shot deal. The art exhibition sounded a little weak. Even the support letters didn't jump-out and grab you.'You don't get anything for nothing in this life', my mother used to say. But what could I offer in return? I got some friends together, brain-stormed through a couple six packs, then we got it.

"WHY DON'T YOU TELL THEM YOU'LL

CYCLE THE RICKSHAW ACROSS CANADA?"

It was as easy as that, and until today, I hadn't given it another thought. End of phone call, I hurriedly took off to my friends bike shop and my rendezvous with karma.

Holy shit! I was gob-smacked. The rickshaw stretched from here to eternity. The intervening years had not only shortened my memory but its size. Somewhere along the line, I'd conveniently blocked out the truth. I had completely forgotten they had one gear, weighed nearly two hundred pounds when empty and could do a pretty good imitation of an 'eskimo roll' when attempting 90 degree turns. Back then rickshaws were no more than three-wheeled projectiles, more to be missed than observed. What had I let myself in for?

Chapter 2
No Pain No Gain

It was 7:30 a.m. I had just finished a condemned man's breakfast of limp toast and lumpy porridge. Outside the rain was pelting down. Curbs had turned into mini-waterfalls and streets into rapids. My brain said let's go, but my body wouldn't budge. Bernie was not a happy camper. I was, as we North America's put it, psyched out. For sixty minutes I stayed glued to the spot. I was excusing myself. Too much rain. Too much traffic. One last cigarette. I was just beginning to enjoy the misery when the rain stopped. The sun popped out and the streets started to steam.

It was 9:30 a.m.by the time I found Victoria's famous MILE 0 signpost marking the beginning of the Trans Canada Highway. The're were no media in attendance, no Trans Canada groupies to talk to, or early morning joggers to wave at. I didn't dip my toe into the Pacific, break a glass of champagne over the rickshaw, or ask for God's blessing. If I was to feel special, it didn't happen. The 6000 plus kilometers I would have to cycle to the finish line hadn't even registered. I couldn't even think past the next bend, let alone Newfoundland. The whole morning had been a non-event. I took out my camera, set its timer, focused in on MILE 0, sat on my rickshaw, said 'cheese' for the record, then peddled away.

My hope of a wind-in-your-hair, carefree trip across Canada didn't even make it to the suburbs. A

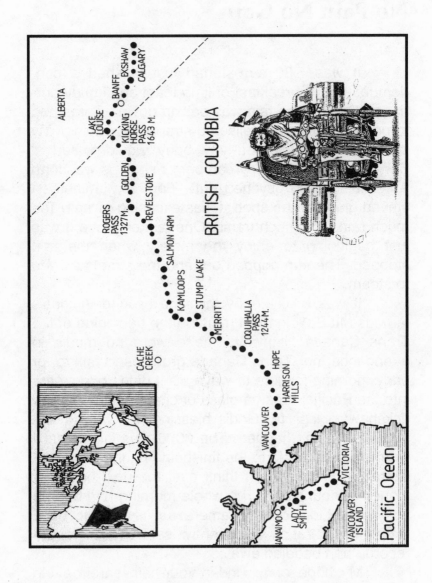

lethal combination of weight, speed and rain made breaking almost impossible. I mounted curbs, ran a light, almost decapitated a pedestrian, and when a truck materialized from nowhere, almost lost it. It was one of those 'Punch and Judy' kind of mornings. I didn't know whether to laugh, cry, or take a valium.

By mid afternoon, I was dismounting at the slightest gradient and by Cobble Hill, I had spent more time pulling than peddling. I was now hearing from muscles, I never knew existed and others of being rudely awakened. My back was creased with pain and a rope burn marked the spot over my shoulder where I pulled the bike. 'No Pain- No Gain', that's what my mother told me. Remembering her words now were of little comfort. Even a masochist has his threshold and I was on borrowed time. Then a car stopped and out popped a turban.

We are all horders by nature. Most people have outward signs like stamp collectors and for others it may be the attic real-estate of their childhood memories or a garage full of nicknacks. My collection is less tangible. It's not based on a credit rating, investment or nostalgia. I collect stories. Not other people's, but my own. I don't know who installed the inbuilt antenna that guides me through life or what powers the magnet that draws me into it, but the end result is never boring.

"Hello old boy, my name is Sammy. Can I take a picture of you with your rickshaw?"

Sammy fell somewhere between a Sumo wrestler in size and an Oxford Don in diction. East Indian by birth, he was your typical Punjabi Sikh; overly large, overly hospitable, and overly noisy.

Apparently he'd seen me earlier in the day on his way home, recognized the rickshaw for what it was and decided I would make the ideal family outing.

"We have thousands of these rickshaws back home in the Punjab, but your's is the first I have seen in Canada, I hope you don't mind. I have brought my family out to see it". Then followed the inevitable....

"You're doing what?"

"I'm cycling it across Canada." Two words, 'across Canada' suddenly elevated me from a mere crazy to that of celebrity status.

"You must meet my family."

Within minutes I was surrounded by a wall of questions. Adjit, Adjay, Panjim, Sanjay, Sonya, and Raja. The guy was a veritable sperm bank of off-spring. I was beginning to feel like a roadside politician, pressing flesh and posing for pictures. Thank God the little monsters soon bored of me. After all, I wasn't the main attraction.

"Daddy Gee. Can we ride on Mr Howgate's rickshaw?"

Sammy deflected the question with the ease of a first class defence lawyer.

"You will have to ask, Mr Howgate".

I had neither the energy or the heart to refuse. I am not very good father material. I nodded my head, stepped back, crossed my fingers and the fight began.

"I want to be driver."

"No, it's my turn".

They fought over everything. Soon both bells were blazing, brakes were strained to the limit and all mirrors had been turned every which way but the right one. Sanjay was screaming; Adjay name calling;

Panjim was on top of Adjit; Raja, too small to reach anything higher than a hub-cap, was fiddling with the air valves and Sonya had turned into a one-woman molting machine, stripping tassels by the handful. Anything that was neither screwed-in, nailed-down nor sealed with duct-tape was being dismantled. Then a truce was called.

"Can we offer you some food, Mr Howgate?"

It wasn't so much an invite as a command. Sammy's wife had quietly converted a small plot of grass into a veritable smorgasbord board of sliced meats, cheeses, diced vegetables and bread. I couldn't ask for a better end-of-the-day experience. Sammy's family had entered my life like fine wine. They had filled my stomach, massaged my heart and left me thirty minutes later, more than a little light-headed. I now felt relaxed. For the first time, I could appreciate the opal blue ocean corridor called the Georgia Strait, its maze of dark green islands and the mainland barrier of snowcapped mountains, I would soon have to cross.

I reached Ladysmith by nightfall. I had completed the last 20 kilometers in just over two hours and felt played out. I chose an open field to camp, rolled out my ground sheet and slept under the stars.

I woke up with rocks in my feet and a rear end so tender that every movement translated into pain. I was getting the electric shock treatment and the more I tried to alter my saddle position, the more painful it got.

I made Nanaimo in double-quick time, but missed the first ferry due to bad planning. I missed the second to stupidity and the third left me holding a phone waiting for a, transatlantic link-up with my parents. The comedy of errors got no better on the mainland. Rush hour was in full swing. Vancouver could wait. I swung north, followed the Whistler Route 99 and chose a beautifully wooded cove near Horseshoe Bay to camp for the night. So far, so good.

The sun had turned into an orange ball. Mozart was in the air and I could hear the distinctive chink of fine china. This was not your average neighbourhood cove. On all sides, half hidden in lush groves of pine, with ocean views that only money can buy, were the rich and famous. I was sandwiched in between a rooftop jacuzzi, a cathedral of glass and a health-nut chanting mantras. I had the best seat in the house and the last one to see the sun set. I drifted off with the light, and then the fun started.......

Holy Shit !

The noise was too close for comfort.

'Who's there?'

The sound got stuck somewhere between my voice box and my clacker. I was scared stiff. It wasn't the unseen noises that frightened me, but the local four-legged neighborhood watch variety. Rottwielers aren't bred for their intelligence and owners don't keep them around for their pet-like qualities. I'd already witnessed one take its owner out for a jog and at least half a dozen more penned-up roadside like living crime deterrents. This looked like the kind of neighbourhood that released their flesh-eating canines first and picked up the bones later.

The sounds were driving me crazy. A rustlel; a moan; a whimper. I took it for ten minutes, then curiosity got the upper hand. I was down wind. I assessed my chances of being scented as nil and spotted as unlikely. I took off along the beach on all fours, picked up a piece of driftwood for protection and crawled up to the sounds.

Oh No! The picture was unmistakable. The position almost impossible.The noises I had taken for animals, were instead, a pair of hot and horny teenagers on the make. Embarrassed, I left.

'Lion's Gate Bridge'. With a name like that, I should have known better. I could have continued down Marine Drive, bypassed the bridge, boarded the C.P.R. ferry at the Third Street Terminal and entered Vancouver at a more leisurely pace but no, Bernie wanted to greet it head-on. I wanted to see the downtown skyline like a picture postcard. I wanted to see Vancouver's famous backdrop of mountains. Take an early morning cycle through Stanley Park, and get a bird's eye view of the weekend yacht races in English Bay.

I could have changed my mind at the first hint of the bridge's gradient or have turned back when four lanes turned into two. I was a quarter of the way across the bridge's footpath when the reality of my situation struck home. One of the bridge's main vertical steel support beams dropped straight through the path, cutting it in half and forming four fenced-in ninety degree turns. No problem for two-wheelers, a piece of cake for your pedestrian, but impossible for a three-wheeled taxi-cab from Pakistan. There were only two choices. Enter the rat race or sprout wings and fly above it. Luckily it was lunch hour. Commuters were migrating west out of town and the east bound lanes were clear.I was over the hump and heading down the other side of the bridge when I heard the first comment.

"Get off the fucking road...."

It was a none too friendly motorist. I wasn't exactly a hit with the truckers, either. I was getting blasted from both directions. By now, I was an accident waiting to happen and when a helicopter appeared, hovered, then pocked a lens out, it was a safe bet that I would end up on the evening news or in a jail cell. I knew I was breaking the law. But, I had no choice. I was on the wrong side of the fence and it wasn't until I passed the last bridge support that the fence disappeared and I could rejoin once again, the footpath. Twenty minutes later, I had exchanged the narrow confines of Lion's Gate Bridge for the freedom of Stanley Park's spacious bicycle trails.

A...oof, A...oof, A...oof, A...oof, A...oof

It was a shark attack. They approached at speed, shot past like oversized bullets, then descended the hill away from me like a dozen jet black hot air balloons. These cyclists weren't your average weekend plodders, these were off-the-seat, ass-in-the-air big league speedsters. You couldn't have done a better job body fitting their spandex if you had poured liquid flesh into them. And complete with 'Darth Vadar' sunglasses and aerodynamic helmets, they formed a group fashion statement on wheels that begged more than a second look.

I followed their trail of banana peels and power bar wrappers until exiting the park on Beach Avenue. By now, I was tired and hungry. I meandered my way down Bute Avenue, took a left on Hastings and before I knew it, I was in Gastown.

"Got a dime, mate" Looking down at him, crossed-legged on the pavement, reminded me of the sixties generation, of those who sailed far into the Bermuda Triangle of sex, drugs and rock and roll and never returned, but then looks can be deceiving. His opening lines had been a knee jerk reaction. A kind of masonic handshake that street people use to separate them from us.

"Is that contraption your's man?" I nodded. The guy was in awe and so were his buddies.News spread like wild-fire. Street people came from as far afield as the bus terminal to pay their respects. After all, I had in my possession a panhandler's dream, a gimmick.

By early evening, I had been passed down into the inner circle. I was amazed at Gastown's potpourri of transient guests, its artists, its musicians, and con-men. I had met privately educated drop-outs, street-wise runaways, a pharmaceutical bad tripper and been entertained by a brass band army of spiritualists, Time just flew by, then, just as the evening's body trade hit the streets, I met Tom.

Tom, I was told, had been around as long as the cobble streets and was just as craggy. He was Hasting's musician-in-residence and top of the pavement pecking order."This is my corner", Tom said, "the best in Gastown", and he meant it. "The town's trying to license us all. It's crap, but it pays the bills." In his own words, he classed himself as the 'pulse of Vancouver', an anti-hero who told it like it was. Put words to music and sang out his message to anyone within earshot. You couldn't help but notice the guy.

Giraffe-like legs, salt and pepper bearded and a gravel voice that only a two-pack a day man could cultivate. He had that character age brings to all of us, but showed considerable signs of having carried them from birth, with a pickle jar chin, mainsail ears, a nose like a trigonometry problem and fiery brown eyes that only years of street encounters could ignite. "We musicians need a healthy downtown core." There was a tone of nostalgia in Tom's voice. Downtowns had changed much in the last decade. The tepid climate of British Columbia had lent itself to a multitude of copycats and Tom had been just one of many fighting for space on Vancouver's streets. Warm temperatures have a way of bringing these freelancers out of society's woodwork, but the advent of the new anesthetic environments were killing the old ones fast.

Tom's downfall, as he puts it, started in the seventies when indoor shopping malls became the norm, and designated areas for gathering, had finally nailed down his coffin. Airports were too distant, railway stations demoted and bus stations, too well policed for his liking. A changing tide of social behaviour had left him high and dry. Bustling sidewalks had been his world and when in 1980 they all but disappeared, he went on a five-year hiatus. Then, in the mid eighties, Japanese hordes invaded the mainland. They didn't carry guns, but blank cheques and cameras. Overnight Gastown was spruced-up, cobbled and given back its character. Tourists started to flood the pavements. Tom found himself relocated to Hastings, given a performer's license and handed a new lease of life as one of Gastown's permanent attractions. "You wouldn't believe how many Japs want their picture taken with me", he said with a laugh.

I left Tom with a gathering crowd. His voice was hoarse and his movements stilted. A glass of water appeared. He gripped it with both hands, placed it on his mouth and drained it in one go. Again his fingers curled around the frets, motionless. No change in rhythm. The sounds emanating were like a mantra, not upbeat but monotonous. The crowd stayed only minutes and were leaving as I peddled away, then....

"Hey, that's him. That's Tom."

I couldn't believe my ears. I glanced back. Tom was surrounded by a new crowd. To some he may have been boring, pitiful even. But watching his dancing eyes, the way he animated his words, it was obvious that others looked upon him as a street-wise guru.

There's nothing more sobering than leaving a city at 5:00 a.m. No echoes, nothing but open roads, robotic traffic lights and empty intersections.

In the suburbs alarms were going-off; lights turning on. Early morning risers were out for walks, and some noses squashed against glass, squinting through glazed eyes to catch the first rays of dawn.

It took a day and a half cycling to reach Hope. I chose highway 7 over highway 1 and was rewarded with some spectacular views of the Fraser River. Both days were sunny, cloudless, with only a hint of wind. I was hitting a rhythm. My back didn't hurt as much and I didn't fight with the saddle any more. I still had to pull more than peddle, but a mountaineering harness converted with padded shoulder straps worked like a charm. In Victoria, I had pared down essentials to the bone. Gone was my spare stove, as was the shotgun

I had brought along for bears, and half my wardrobe of clothes. I had exchanged duffel bags of storage for a tarpaulin ground sheet and my tent for a bivisac. My plan was to travel light, camp under the stars whenever possible and call on local hospitality whenever it rained. This wasn't my first long distance cycle trip or my first without a tent. Meeting people is the name of the game in my book, scenery comes a distant second and travelling without a tent is a main ingredient. It adds an element of vulnerability and luck to my trips. Where should I stay tonight? What view should I sleep with? In the real world, I wouldn't say boo to a moose, but on the road, I'm as brazen as they come and not past knocking on a door or two during bad weather. In the past, I've slept in everything from church to jail cell. From barn to mansion. You name it and I've either slept in or above it.

When I left Hope, the sun had not yet popped its head above the mountains and I was chilled to the bone. I was now on the east side of the Fraser river. Today's plan was to take the more direct route to Kamloops on the recently constructed Highway 5 over the Coquihalla Pass, save two days and take one off.

Within the hour, I was boiling and without doubt would have been toasted if not for my harness. Steep wasn't the word to describe the gradient. It was sheer back-breaking hell. I didn't need eyes to see. There was only one direction; up, and the high-pitched grate of approaching traffic down gearing was a dead giveaway. Under normal circumstances I could have rested more often, appreciated the view, but it's difficult to be appreciative when nightfall is just around the corner. There wasn't even a postage stamp of grass to rest on, let alone shelter for the night, and it was only going to get worse. Ahead peaks tapered, vee'd sharply and dropped like walls to a pass borded in white. In the eight hours since I had left Hope, the weather had swung from chilled to hot, dry to wet and now there was frost in the air. I was beginning to resemble a sweaty pig with a touch of the shivers more than your epic explorer. Then it snowed.

I had no sooner passed through an avalanche tunnel when I entered into a thick cloud of snow flakes. I could hardly see my hand in front of my face. I stopped, put back on every stich of clothing I had, bit into a chocolate bar and gunned it. The road was tilting. Suddenly a breeze slapped my face.Clouds gave way to a battery of lights and the road levelled. Ahead were Coquihalla's toll booths. I had made it. I could feel the warm glow of a heated room. The smell of fresh coffee and,if I was lucky, shelter for the night.

It's not easy to describe the effect that the first sight of a wild animal has on a none too brave author. It's like taking your four year old on a surprise visit to the 'Temple of Doom'. I felt a vaulting thrill combined with a strong desire to start crying and crawl into the nearest goffer hole.

I'd just left Coquihalla's summit. I had spent a glorious night of cabin hospitality and felt on top of the world. The early morning air pinched my face, but I didn't care, all trails led down. I was taking a roadside leak, too preoccupied to notice anything and at first the bear didn't even register. It was too small, too distant and too unlike what I imagined a bear to be, but it

W. Reger

kept on coming.

To this day I can't put any sequence to the events. I know it stopped, stuck its nose in the air, then bolted, but what happened next is a blur. Was there one or two? Did I run into it or away from it ? Did the bear try to escape or attack? Somewhere along the line we crossed. He had shoulders like the rock of Gibraltar, paws as big as your head and an ass so big it blocked out the sun. I was frozen and fried at the same time. I remember falling and tasting the grass. I remember arms flailing like windmills and screams with no sound. I got up covered in dirt. My knees and elbows were grazed, but no teeth marks. I was more embarrassed than frightened. I brushed myself down. Checked that no one was looking, then peddled away like 'Cool Man Luke'. Twenty minutes later the shakes set in.

At Merritt, I branched off the Coquihalla high-way and took the old Route 5A through cattle country. I didn't give a damn if I ever saw the mountains again. I wanted out of bear country. I didn't want to see another tree, dark shadow or blade of grass. The sur-rounding hills on Route 5A were too low to catch water and too high to irrigate. These were the bald hills of open range, with barely enough food to sustain cattle let alone the lush plant life bears feed on. That night, I camped on the shores of Stump Lake. I was on a piece of arid ground borded on two sides with water and on one by road. I was on red alert. I couldn't shake the thought of bears out of my head. All night they taunted me. I was up and down like a yo-yo and by dawn I was just about brave enough to sleep.

I started off the day badly. My eyes were double glazed and so looked the road. I missed the first bend, skidded, then broadsided a parked pick-up.

"Ya, all right?"

Its owner had not even bothered to check for dents.

"John's my name"

I introduced myself, apologized for the accident and told him where I had come from and where I was heading to. Then asked the wrong question.

"Do you farm around here?"

In this neck of the woods farming was obviously a dirty word.

"The only farmers you'll see in these parts wear horn-rimmed glasses, use words like organic, and are too educated for their own good."

John came straight out of the pages of a kid's cowboy book. Lean and hungry like a stick of chewing gum. He had the facial features that broke into a Rocky Mountain route map whenever he smiled. A man of few words, he picked his way round sentences like some people do over water, then the bear story broke him up.

"I fought it with my bare hands."At times like these, a good lie is better than the embarrassing truth."I beat the snot out of it". I couldn't keep a straight face and by the time I finished the story on dirty underwear, we were kindred spirits. Then, for some strange reason, children came up.

"What, no kids?" He was genuinely shocked. Family life meant every thing to him. It went to the core of his manhood, gave his life meaning and anyone who didn't fit the same mould, he felt sorry for. "You're missing out on something, Bernie",he continued. "My little buggers keep me young, especially the grand-children." We were from the same generation, yet poles apart. John, was a high school drop-out at 14, married at 16 and was a father twice over before crashing his teens. He'd started life half way through, then played catch-up but hadn't regretted a second. All his friends had the same history. School, marriage, children. Life was simple. He wore his character like the clothes on his back. From boot to hat, they had that worn-in look. A practical statement that fitted him like a glove, with muscles built for work, not as a fash-ion statement. "Look me up in Loops". His invite was so matter-of-fact that I almost missed it. There were no time tables asked for. "Sometime today or tomor-row, if you want." Food wasn't even mentioned, yet I knew it would be offered and a night between clean sheets was never in doubt. We parted at 10:00 a.m., met again on his doorstep at 4:00 p.m. and continued where we had left off, as if old friends. We drank and lied through the night. The bear drowned sometime between sunset and sunrise. Alcohol can do that to a man.

I left Kamloops on Highway 1, although you would never have guessed it. Traffic was sparse at best and with the exception of an occasional mini-con-voy headed by logging trucks, I had the Trans Canada Highway all to myself. The road now followed a lazy curve caused by the South Thompson River. It was blisteringly hot. I had now covered over 400 kilome-ters, averaged over 60 kilometers per day and felt as fit as a fiddle. I was a lean, mean, peddling machine. I had transferred my pink layers of city fat into the taut wind-burnt look of a vagabond. Leg muscles were rock hard and my bum had toughened under a new layer of skin. My Newfie blush had expanded in the last few days and now took in both arms and legs and today it was getting the jock-strap treatment. In just over one week, I had converted flesh into muscle, increased my life expectancy by years and gained a healthy taste for B.C. beers.

I made Salmon Arm in a breeze, camped under the stars and duplicated the distance next day to Revelstoke.

'I once met a girl in Revelstoke'. I really did. It was back in the days when I was a hormonally imbalanced divorcee. I met Katie playing touch-football in a Toronto park. She was straight out of U of T; naive, expectant and full of life. She turned me onto the Argonauts, indoor activities of the sweaty variety and of all things, the railways. Katie was your stereotypical child of Trudeau Nationalism. She wanted to taste, touch and smell Canada first hand and while her classmates were globe trotting around the world, her passport to adventure was a coast-to-coast railway ticket.

My first taste of the Trans Canada Railway system came via a 16mm film. It was during the '50s post-war flood of immigration. The new worlds of the British Commonwealth were competing for English workers to expand their horizons. Town Hall film shows were the norm and school gymnasiums the captured audience of future generations. South Africa built its theme around its gold and diamond mines, its wildlife and

Capetown's Table Top Mountain. Australia sold its 'Outback', New Zealand its sheep and Canada centred its pitch on the Trans Canada Railway. They took us on a thirty minute journey from Atlantic to Pacific, from the polar bear country of Hudson Bay to the fruit orchards of the Okanagan. The railway linked not only Canada's vast geographical differences from Plains to Rockies, but its rich cultural heritage. It seemed then that the railway was as much part of Canada as the Maple Leaf is today.

A train journey across Canada, especially for new arrivals like myself in the '70s, was a unique experience. Moving slowly as it did, loosely wrapped around time tables. Its appeal was not its comfort, cost or menu, but in its old world hospitality. Those who partook, travelled in limbo, no longer leaving, but not yet arrived. It was a unique way of scratching the surface of Canadian life. The revolving door of passengers with names ending in OV and SKY, the French-English connection and the diverse scenery. 'You have to have stamina,' as Katie said, 'but it's well worth the effort.' Her enthusiasm planted a germ. Now it was my turn.

I last saw Katie boarding a train at Tornoto's Union Station. Her ticket was for Montreal, Fredricton, Halifax and St. John's. I never found out if she made it all the way or what she'd learned. That was fifteen years ago. Today there's no coast to coast rail link, only road. The politics of profit had cut, stripped and killed off most of the old routes. I stopped in Revelstoke only long enough to salute the ending of this era, to walk back through nostalgia and to see if I could recapture some of Katie's spirit.

From Revelstoke it was all uphill. Some people say that mountains spoil the view, but that's only true if you live in their valleys. My first real taste of mountain cycling, and I'd underestimated the whole day First, I never seemed to be dressed right for the occasion. In eight hours I'd experienced four seasons in one. The weather had, in turn, burnt my nose, drenched me from head to foot and now, under a setting sun, was freezing my butt off. And if all that wasn't enough, I had been peddling on empty ever since entering Glacier National Park, and that was three hours ago. I'd based my whole day on a half way top-up at their camp store only to find a 'Closed for the Season' sign. Now, I was suffering from a touch of the 'runs', brought on by drinking too much of that healthy pristine ice-cold mountain water, so thank God for pit stops.

Taking breaks, or pit stops as I like to call them, are the closest I get to a religious experience when travelling. They are to be looked forward to, guarded jealously and to be chosen with care. To the masses a pit stop is not a luxury but a downright necessity. A time to relieve oneself, lubricate the itch at the back of one's throat and take a bite of energy. But, just because it's a necessity doesn't mean you have to be spartan. While my fellow travellers are fighting for space at the roadside 'look-out', peeling out their children and eating cheese spread sandwiches, I am looking for that elusive patch of solitary comfort. A room with a view would help but it's not essential. I look for a clump of trees, a slash of sun and a natural armchair of undergrowth to rest on. Today, I found none. Roger's Pass had turned into a wind tunnel of snow pellets and hypothermia. My blood turns into sludge in double quick time if bared to the cold for prolonged periods. Losing an appendage to frost bite might do wonders for book sales, but reproduction nipped in the bud isn't my idea of self sacrifice. I completed the last few miles in a yogic trance, stopped at the first signs of life, relieved myself, then bedded down aptly enough in the clinical, semi-heated environment of the summit's tile floored toilets.

Have you ever gazed in wonder at the 'Northern Lights', slipped down the 'Milky Way' or traced in a constellation? Well, I haven't. I don't mind being hypnotized by a rising moon or courting a beautiful lady under a jet black sky lit up by stardust. That's not to say I take it all for granted. A meteor shower is definitely worth writing home about and eclipses are worth the price of admission. But the point I'm making, the main event that night and every night you're seven thousand feet above sea level and the skies are clear, is not one of your natural wonders, but man-made. It started with Yuri and now they criss-cross the horizon like so much illuminated garbage. Satellite spotting is a rare art and I love it. I do believe, some nights, I see them wobble. Once I swore a satellite stopped and did a 'U' turn, or was it an Ultra-light airplane? Tonight's sky was absolutely amazing. It didn't have the fullness one experiences on the plains of Saskatchewan or Manitoba, or if viewed at sea, but what it lacked in broad screen panorama, it more than made up for in clarity. I could almost reach up and touch them. Spot the differences between Soyus and Apollo and count the moon's craters. Of course, I exaggerate, but when

you are at high altitude, breathing thin air is like sip-
ping expensive champagne. Its bubbles can work
wonders on the brain and exaggerations come easily
to a dreamer. Needless to say, I slept like a log that
night, woke at the first light on a power surge and set
off in overdrive.

Pssssssssss.... After only one mile the bubble
burst. So much for the bright start. My first puncture. If
you have,every tried to change a car tire with a screw
driver, you'll understand my problem. That's not to say
I hadn't brought along a repair kit. I had all the latest
types of patches from glue to fusion, even two spare
tires and one inner tube, but there's a mile and a half
difference between a normal ten speed and a rickshaw. I had punctured the front tire. To get it off, I
would have to unbolt four support struts and an ornate
guard, then try to pry an almost molded tire from its
heavy duty rim. What I had was a high-tech tool kit.
What I really needed was a jack hammer, a chain saw
and the Koran. It took me ninety minutes but I solved
the problem. I found a rock, used an adjustable
wrench I found the previous day by the roadside and
all my spoons and forks, were now bent.

It was ten o'clock. The early morning sun was
playing peek-a-boo and so was my mood. The flat
newly paved summit road was soon replaced by the
constant twists, turns and dips of descent and the
recent patchwork quilt of fill-ins caused by frost made
the road extremely bumpy. Everywhere there was evidence of avalanches. Deep cuts opened onto treeless
lines of rock, and roadside fall-out was becoming a
constant problem. Even rain-evaporated bone-dry sur-

faces were of no consolation. Thick mantles of fog obscured vision and muffled sounds, leaving it almost impossible to judge vehicle distance and direction. Twice I was caught in 'avalanche tunnels'. I felt like a trapped rat. Everywhere were the elements of danger. The noise was deafening. Adjustment from natural to incandescent tunnel light - blinding and with escape-proof curbs - nowhere to go. On one occasion the tail-gate suction from a sixteen-wheeler almost tore the handlebar from my fingers. I hated the bloody tunnels. They were bicycle death-traps and had it not been for the steep roadside drop-offs, I would have gladly by-passed every one of them.

I made the descent into Golden by early after-noon, calmed my nerves with a Big Mac, indulged my sweet tooth with a milk shake then started the slow climb into Yoho National Park.

It's hard to believe that there is a hide-and-seek policy that follows tourist routes through the province, but there is. It starts innocently enough with a provin-cial lack of rock graffiti, moves onto strategically placed camera-ready 'look-out' stops, and ends dis-cretely hidden behind 'wood-cut' warning signs that forbid roadside cutting for personal use within thirty meters of the road. It wasn't until I had risen above the Columbia River, above its broad valley and above the camouflaged corridor of roadside trees, that I could see the real picture. Clear-cut Logging has not only scarred and eroded British Columbia's mountain sides, but opened deep wounds in its psyche. The bad guy in this scenario, if you are Greenpeace, is the log-ging industry and if you're a logger, it's Greenpeace. Ever since the earliest days of the fur trade, loggers have worked on the principle of infinite resource. In those early days you could have excused this belief, but today it's downright irresponsible.

I believe there's a sanctity in great forests like that of old cathedrals, but we don't save old cathedrals and I haven't met many people who wanted to save them only to leave them empty. There are no easy answers. The pulp and paper industry is one of the province's largest employers, and at the other end of the spectrum Eco Tourism (the new buzz word for the nineties, used to promote everything from the fig leaf to the butterfly) is quickly climbing the same totem pole of employment. Both camps have powerful allies, both share the common belief that they are right and the other wrong. Somewhere in the common sense middle are the normal folk; the poor buggers that will inherit this mess and have to live with its consequences long after its news has been relegated to the back pages. I don't usually allot a great deal of time to these matters, but then, I don't usually find my nose pushed up against its window. It was a depressing sight. Valley after valley. Hill top after hill top. A criss-cross of dirt track roads in a treeless wilderness and by the time I made camp I was downright miserable, then David walked into my thoughts.

"Aren't you supposed to peddle this thing?" Apparently David had been out exercising his 'First Nation' status, doing a little illicit hunting, seen me staggering up the road with the rickshaw in tow, taken me for a crazy do-gooder promoting a cause and dropped in for a little leg pulling.

"There was a time when I knew this area like the back of my hand; could tell time from the sun's angle and could walk bare foot for miles. Now, I wear hiking boots, travel by car, tell time by a watch and don't go anywhere without a route map." Odd-job man by trade, part-time guide and occasional school story teller by profession, David soon had me in stiches.His life was a CATCH 22 of contradictions. Born on a reservation, but educated in an English-speaking Catholic school. David somehow fell between the cracks of society and in that respect we had much in common. He was a ray of light in an otherwise depressing day and when he offered to cook the evening meal our friendship was sealed. He'd enjoyed my company and in return, I was to enjoy his cooking. Soon a whole tin of 'spam' was sizzling. For ten minutes, I watched David prepare a full meal of spam, onions and beans in the same sooty-black pan he must have used on countless occasions. Then, in less time than it took to bat an eye-lid, polished it off. Pans were scraped and plates licked clean. His meal had filled a niche and his freshly ground coffee, the rest. His cooking was no gastronomic feat, but cooked on an open fire, and barbecued in the natural smoke of balsam had no equals. Then out popped the dreaded question.

"Can I ride your bike?"

I know, I shouldn't have. I had made a promise to myself not to let anyone ride it and I meant anyone. Touch it, yes. Sit on the saddle, fiddle with it, but no, no, no, to riding. I tried to block out the memory of frying spam, the taste of beans and the roaring fire I was enjoying.

"Pretty please." He had that 'kiddy's plea' look in his eyes. "Can I? Can I? Can I?"

I tried to say no, but the word came out like a limp squid. "Well....... I don't really........ OK." He was up and off like a shot and on the saddle before I could change my mind.

"Whowee." He had no idea. I doubt if he'd ever been on a two-wheeler let alone three. The Indian in him had got the upper hand. He was all enthusiasm with nowhere to go but down. For one awful second, I watched my whole trip bounce off a rock, lurch, then disappear over a bank.

"Are you OK?" What I really meant was the bike. The two of them reappeared moments later. One looked wet, slightly scratched, but none the worse for it. The other was just beaming.

"That was great, man. I think I've got the hang of it. Can I have another go?" It didn't take too much effort the second time around to say, no. I wasn't up to a replay. Game finished, we both sat back around the fire gypsy-like, toasting our knees. Then, without a by your leave, he was gone.

Yoho National Park has something for everyone. It doesn't matter whether you're a drive-through sightseer, day trekker or month-long wilderness junkie. It has a mood to suit every personality. It's a 24-hour, 365 day a year forecaster's nightmare. The weather, like its scenery, is totally unpredictable. There's a story round every corner and cloud formations you wouldn't believe. Deep valleys drop into boiling water, empty into slow moving rivers, then come to rest in lakes of opal green. Mountains rise like buttresses of rock, plateau and open onto fields of alpine color. It's a continuous visual experience. An 'Alice through the looking glass', but through it all there's the ever-present feeling of being watched. Big horn sheep graze roadside and stop on queue to be photographed. Mountain goats clatter across rocks like groups of threadbare refugees and the majestic, many-pointed elks hardly acknowledge passing cars. Who can forget the sight of an eagle soaring skyward or wouldn't give their back teeth to see a three hundred and fifty pound grizzly bear or a moose rising above the early morning fog. I had conquered three passes; the Coquihalla, Roger's and now Kicking Horse. They all gave more than they took. The air was crisp, clean and invigorating. The waters pristine and ice cold. You may not be closer to God in the Rockies, but you sure increase your chances of escaping the devil of pollution. It's a kind of 'Stomping Tom's' playground where Mounties still wear red and the young "have a nice day" boys and girls at the tourist information booths really do mean what they say. Over the years I have experienced Asia's overpowering Himalayas in Nepal, trekked through Europe's Alps to the 'Sounds of Music' and seen Mount McKinley's golden pyramid on one of those rare cloud-free days, but nothing comes close to the unique Canadian Rockies for diversity. Where else can you find McDonalds competing on a level playing field for custom with abundant wild life? Where else can you buy a hot dog, get your Nikon repaired and see bear, beaver and porcupine all in the same day. I had turned, in just a few short weeks, into the bicycling version of a mountain climber. I was on a high. Bragging rights were in my pocket and I had letters to write. I passed through the 'Great Divide' archway; took the now standard 'That's me, next to the...........' picture for the boys back home and for just a moment thought about spending one more night in the mountains. Then a sign warning of garbage, bears and what to do if attacked changed my mind.

Like a big dipper the road dropped into my belly. Within seconds, I entered the world of speed. Who cares about helmets, injury or life expectancy when life hits the fast lane. My eyes glued to the road, my mind entered the make-believe world of road races. Spectators cheered, animals roared and scenery passed by unnoticed. I duelled with imaginary cars, surprised slow moving trucks and by the time I bellied out on the Parkland's Highway, I was in heaven. Ahead, Mount Richardson rose like a stern nude statuette. I was out of the snow belt. The air was full of scent. Yellows and blues borded the road and insects whined. To the south east a huge tidal wave of rock rose almost perpendicular from a green carpet of ferns and to the west a fresh coating of snow subdued the edges I had just left. I was now only forty five kilometers from the Columbia Icefield; the birth place of three great rivers; the Saskatchewan, Athabasca and Columbia. Together they embrace over a third of the continent and empty into three different oceans. It felt awesome just being there.

Little Big Man
Chapter 3

. I am not a large man, but occasionally some-thing inside me bursts and adrenaline levels shoot up a thousand percent. Neck hairs tingle and my head spins. It turns me into Jesus and Lucifer all at the same time and is one of the main reasons I travel solo. The descent of Kicking Horse Pass had been the straw that broke the camel's back. I was over the edge. Like passing your finals, I could now afford to go crazy, explode, unwind, then relax into its memory. I had entered the Rockies naive, ill-prepared, but passed through with flying colors. From now on, it would be all down hill. The Atlantic was still over four thousand kilometers away, but the worst was over. Little did I know then, but the Rockies were only the beginning. I now knew what pain was like and although it hadn't registered, it would become a recurring bedfellow in the months to come.

There are times when I hate doing what I do. The travel; the fitness bug; being able to pack up and go whenever I please. Oh, to be normal. I'm the envy of most people I meet. 'I wish I could travel like you'. If only they knew. Some days I crave the wifely thing. A mortgage to tie me down and children to live out my dreams. Relationships on the road usually start in the middle, rush to the end and miss out the friendship stage. An old friend once commented on my girl-friends as 'Instant orgasm without baggage', but occa

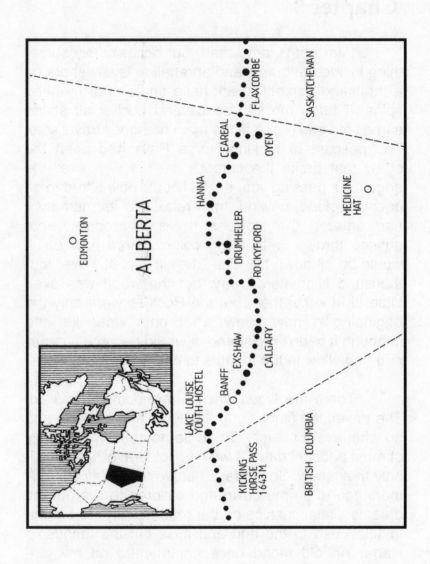

sionally, very rarely in fact, I meet someone so different, so young that friction never enters the equation.
The brakes of physical attraction are applied without
thinking, and trust and friendship is never questioned.

I had just stoked up the fire in a make-shift
sauna, steamed up the room and was stripped and
ready to bleed sweat, when its door opened.

"Oops........ Sorry."

We didn't have time for formal introductions.
She looked in, turned red and bolted. Sixty minutes
later I would meet Dianne again, this time over coffee.

There's just something about youth hostels in
general, and this one in particular, that strip down barriers and make friendships easy to cement. They are
a kind of poor man's Club Med without the staged
events. The Lake Louise Youth Hostel on Highway 1A
was your down and dirty type; where water comes in
buckets, light by kerosene and, being off the bus and
tourist routes, a location passed on more by word of
mouth than your average guide book.

We had arrived on the same day, but that's all
we had in common. Coming from a genteel background of private schools and manicured lawns,
Dianne's - travels until a few days ago - had come
through adventure books, predictable game parks and
the hand-me-down stories of her older sister. Quite
simply, she had come to Alberta to see the wild life,
was too frightened to go out on her own and 'Would I,
Bernie, take her for a ride tomorrow?'

Cycling together that morning, I felt privy to a
new experience. For her it must have been like sex
first time around and for me, reliving it. She had spent

twenty minutes fiddling with her borrowed bike, wanting badly to go, but waiting for me to push her. But once I had made the first move, she was off like a rocket. Every corner was met with wide-eyed anticipation. Every noise with the chance of something new. She skipped over bridges, danced around bends and waltzed up the straights. An elk gave her a casual glance, pricked up its ears at the sound of my rickshaw, then half jumped, half glided out of view. A female white tailed deer, baby in tow, seduced her off her bike. She hiked up her jeans, kicked off her runners and ran bare foot towards them. One time, she sat silently for twenty minutes to catch one glance of a beaver and the next moment was sprinting headlong towards a mountain goat. She held nothing back and as the morning drew to a close, her leash of security I had been entrusted with got longer and longer.

By noon, she had tired. She'd exhausted all questions, overdrawn her bank of energy and squeezed the morning dry of experiences. She just wanted to lay down and dream about it. We stopped near a stream. Her face glowed, but her eyes, tired from searching, were closed. She fell asleep where she sat. I watched her for half an hour. Occasionally her eyes would flutter. A word would fall, a muscle twitch and then she would drop back into her dream.

"You missed the bear," I said jokingly. Her eyes glazed, blinked, then sparkled.

"I bet you didn't see the tiger?" she replied. She had it all inside her from story books again. Fact and fantasy now overlapped and as we cycled back to the youth hostel she fell back into her childhood, talking to animals with clothes, in houses like Alice, wanting never to grow up.

That night we linked arms and went for a walk to a nearby pond, she throwing stones and making wishes and I just glad to be there. She was in love, not with me, but with the picture before her. For one day, I had lived life through her eyes. She had injected a youthful vigour back into my trip and in exchange, I now passed through hers.

"You would make a great uncle, Bernie."

She couldn't have given me a better compliment if she had tried. The day ended all to quickly. I hadn't taken one picture, given in to one promise or exchanged addresses. I didn't need to. I knew in my heart we would meet again; not Dianne, but the feeling she gave me. It was magic.

The following morning, I left before daybreak. For two hours I had the whole road to myself. The Rockies were sleeping. It was that time of day, not yet light, but not dark either. Mountains were still in silhouette and a pre-dawn mist hid the foothills. I was cycling down a telescope of ragged shadows, then slowly the sky coloured. Dark surfaces melted like snow under heat. Rocks turned from jet black to blood red, to orange. Harsh outlines mellowed within minutes, then bleached into a heat haze. I was in a great mood. The Little Big Man inside me was bursting with pride. At my present pace, Calgary was only three days away. I was cycling on Route 1A in the Bow River Valley and there wasn't a hill in sight. By 8:00 a.m. I got a little peckish. I can be proper grumpy without my early morning fix of caffeine, and stopped at the first signs of life.

Should I or shouldn't I? Ahead, I could see a twenty-four hour Truck Stop and just a little further down the road an exit sign for Banff. The guide books say that no visit to the Rockies is complete without the 'Banff Experience'. I flipped a coin, cycled passed the Truck Stop, followed my nose to the first junk food take-out, then sat down just off the main street to watch the floor show.

Banff is to Alberta what Disneyland is to Florida. An adult amusement arcade in a sea of wilderness. It had been against my better judgement to make the detour. First, I had to pass through the ten foot high security fence, built more, I guess, to keep the tourist in than keep the animals out. Banff is a strange mixture of the vulgar and the tranquil. A cocktail that at first sip is bitter, but it grows on you. It's a place where city comforts have been shipped in so that the visitors can taste the wilderness without suffering food poisoning. Where spring water has to be chlorinated and cool mountain air requires the A/C treatment. Here big game hunters shoot with cameras not guns, fight to feed bears and not to run away from them and are parted from their money not by hold-ups, but by inflated prices.

You haven't lived until you have seen a tour bus disgorge a whole tribe of Japanese matchstick look-a-likes weighed down with cameras.Do they do anything else but take pictures? Japanese travel in packs, jog at a trot, and get up at 6:00 a.m. If you don't believe me, stake-out the Vancouver Hilton during tourist season. Japanese take snap shots of everything. Back in Tokyo there must be billions of color slides depicting fire hydrants, manhole covers, pedestrian cross-walks phone booths and the piece-de-resistance, petrol station discount gas prices. "What are the Japanese doing with these pictures?" you may ask. It's also probably a question the Americans should have asked before Pearl Harbour. And what of the Americans, our 'Great to be in Ya' Country' southern neighbours with their 22-gallon Stetsons shading everything from their bleach blond heiresses with teeth that cost thousands to their inflated bellies. And I haven't finished yet. Down the street at your quaint 'Swiss Countryfied Chicken' was a group of Germans in beach attire. The old addage -the bigger the ass, the smaller the shorts- fit them down to a tee. And if you missed spotting their appendages you can sure hear them whispering to each other a block and a half away.

"Over here." I'd been spotted. Suddenly my rickshaw lit up like the fourth of July. Cameras came in from all angles. Pen and paper materialized in front of my face.

"Please, your name, please?"I was now a name, date and file reference to be resurrected as a prize to be shown to women's groups from A to Z. Then the 'Brady Bunch' had arrived. Ten sticky fingers were playing with my bells and another ten were searching for souvenirs. Hello and goodbye.

Sunday bloody Sunday. I had unknowingly entered the bible belt of closure. The highway to Cochrane was deserted. What life there was centred around the occasional spiral. Christendom was in full swing and the sounds of bells filled the air. I felt ripe for conversion. One glass of water, one nibble of chocolate and I was ready to act the repentant sinner, ready to do handstands down the aisle, curse out the devil and talk in tongues if need be.

The Bow Valley was being swept by a chinook. (the peculiar Calgarian weather pattern that localizes hot spots like boils on your neck). It was hotter than hell. A dry west wind had crept up like an intruder. Horizons wobbled. A hazy sheen glazed the road and the smell of burning rubber tore at my nostrils. It must have been eighty degrees in the shade, but felt much hotter. My skin prickled and itched. Moisture drained like a leaky cup and my calorie bank was bare. My batteries were running down fast and the more I tried to pedal forward the more the road held me back. My legs were winding down and a fever seemed to be creeping through my veins. The horizon had stopped. A radio was playing in my head, then out, then in again. A blur shaped, roadside, then folded into a house. I reached it in slow motion. I saw some signs but kept on going. The music started again, then went. First things first, I needed water. A garden hose did the trick, then thoughts of food. My stomach was churning. I had just turned in the direction of the house when a dog appeared, lunged in my direction and nearly tore my arm off.

"Can't you read the signs?" The dog was leashed to a none too pleased owner. I couldn't exactly play dumb. My rickshaw was parked next to his 'Beware of the Dog' sign and I could remember at least three 'Trespass' signs since leaving the highway.

"Get the fuck off my property before I call the police."

"I only wanted............" I couldn't wrap my tongue around the words. Get a grip, Bernie. I was shaking. Emotions rose, flooded my eyes and the gates opened. "I'm sorry........"

There's something about seeing a grown man cry that's both pathetic and persuasive. It's like waving a white flag. Unconditional surrender. The farmer looked totally embarrassed.

"We are a bit isolated out here. You can't be too careful." Then his wife appeared.

"What's going on ?"

What a sight we must have made; me crying my eyes out; him lost in limbo, somewhere between victorious dictator and humanitarian.

"I thought he was one of those rough-necks, we had last week."

You couldn't blame him. With unkempt hair and scraggy beard, I was beginning to look more like a rastafarian than a cross-Canada cyclist. I felt a complete jerk, crying and all. It wasn't that he intimidated me. Far from it, he looked old enough to be my father. It was that feeling of being caught with your hand in the cookie jar. The naughty-boy syndrome, knowing that you were wrong, yet feeling that you were in the right, all in the same breath. I didn't stop shaking until we were all inside. Once again knowledge of my trip opened doors. Apologies were given from both sides and readily accepted. I was treated to a meal of home cooked pea soup and freshly made bread. In return, I filled their minds with adventure, attacked everything put in front of me and accepted every back-slapping praise of my trip like a tickled baby. By the time I left, my emotions had swung one hundred and eighty degrees and so had the weather.

The sky was now evenly divided between black

and blue. Neither day nor night. It hung like a damp water colour, then dropped. Rain, rain and more rain. It came in buckets, stripped me of warmth and left the rickshaw's seat a dam to be filled. Events were crowning in, thick and fast. At the storm's height the sky was pitch black. Lightning strikes bounced everywhere and thunder like depth charges rocked the road. I had detoured back onto the Trans Canada Highway at Cochrane and now every passing car gave me the wash-down treatment. The road had turned into a fast-moving river, and its dips into slow-moving lakes.

By early afternoon the rain had run its course. Clouds were now high in the sky and Calgary was arched by a rainbow. The highway river had drained into a trickle and soon the only evidence that a storm had passed through were the occasional high tide marks of leaves. One hour later the C.N. Tower loomed out of the mist like a giant mushroom and sixty minutes after that, I had entered the 'STRIP'.

The Strip is a uniquely North American invention - a consumer belt of fast-food restaurants, discount gas bars and motels - that takes travellers in tired and hungry at one end, and rolls them out fed, fuelled and rested at the other. Its service for the masses on the run. They are drive-through havens, designed for cars with people in mind and, without both, wouldn't exist. They announce better than any milepost the 'City Limits' and if you can pass through their gauntlet of tacky billboards without stopping once, you are a better man than me. I wasn't about to miss out on a milk shake and KFC's three-piece dinner special looked more than inviting. By the time I had exited down Crowchild Trail, I felt more like a stuffed pig than the lean mean travelling machine I had on entry.

At first glance, Calgary looks like a young kid who has long since outgrown his clothes. It's loud and brash and doesn't mind showing off its dirty underwear in public. It's a mixture of old time 'Y'a have a nice day', hospitality and gold rush vulgarity and it's my favourite city on the continent. It's a place where Country and Western reigns supreme and delicate table manners, like polite conversation, has very little currency. It still brags that men are men and women are expensive. From one end of 9th Avenue to the other, it's wall-to-wall glass, acres of it. It's like every mirror in Canada was bought, shipped out west and plastered onto the buildings. After ten days in the Rockies, Calgary's bright lights put all that healthy exercise into perspective. I couldn't wait to pig-out and indulge in its amusement arcade of entertainment.

I ended up staying four days. A friend of a friend of a friend, one phone call and a bag load of trust on the part of my hosts, and by day's end I was resting in the warm glow of adopted family life. It was a fantastic feeling just to have a shower again, wear freshly laundered clothes and have the privacy of my own room. Within twenty-four hours, I was almost civilized, by thirty-six, I had regained my table manners and by forty-eight, I was downright dilettante, oozing P's and Q's and 'Can, I help with the dishes?' I did the usual tourist things. I visited the zoo, walked through Eaton's, bought souvenirs and went leg-spotting in Bow Valley Park. In fact life was bliss, couldn't have been better, then I had a slight accident.

It was a case of 'David meets Goliath' with a twist. The twenty-one gear titanium feather weight mountain terrier didn't stand a chance. This wasn't one of those kiss and make-up type of bumps; this was a crash - bang wallop, love at first sight, take me to your leader kind of accident. It started with eye contact, a neck twisting double take, a cross road rendezvous, then whacko! The poor kid was thunder-struck. He had eyes only for the rickshaw and when eventually, he found a voice, couldn't stop talking.

"What is IT?"

"Where did you get IT?"

"How much is IT worth?"

"How many speeds has IT got?"

"How heavy is IT?"

'IT' was dominating the conversation and 'IT's owner was getting slightly pissed-off. I was beginning to wish I had reversed over the guy, put him out of his misery, at the very least knocked 'IT' out of his head, then an invite came my way. "Drop by the Hard Rock. Don't forget to bring 'IT' along." Well at least, I was included.

The 'Hard Rock' turned out to be a bike courier hang-out and it wasn't hard to find. Outside, locked nose to tail, every two-wheeler known to man was on display. Mountain bikes overlapped racers. I had to step over a uni-cycle, maneuver around a recumbent and move two single speed clungsters to get in. Some bikes wore their owner's monograms like price tags while others spray painted in vivid primary colours took on a uniqueness all of their own. There were drop bars, up-turns, long horns and droopies with straight cuts and that was only the beginning. Once inside my eyes burned. Colours shouted out from every corner. My pupils bounced from bare flesh to T-shirt to bare flesh again. Multi-coloured knickers and black spandex tights begged to be stroked and wet-look vests all stretched to their limits of design had me wanting to attach my hands to them. Animal magnetism poured into leotards leave little to the imagination. Ass, tits and testicles were on show and you needed a pair of heavy-duty sun glasses just to soften the blow. I'd entered the culture of envy, and boy, was I envious. In entering the coffee bar, I'd gatecrashed a war lords' meeting. 'Nothing like getting some power between your legs'. Sayings were jumping out of mouths like well rehearsed bible teachings and the air was heavy with recruitment. All around tables were filled with 100% natural juice and the spring waters of eternal youth. I was at the cutting edge of a new millennium.

At my table a hormone-stroking young girl in full length wet suit argued the merits of the full length look while opposite a hairy chest framed in a bib suit argued his. Opposite, two young men were almost coming to blows over helmets.The pros and cons over hard versus soft shells were being argued over and chins straps, padding and colour coding discussed in detail. One guy wanted the hockey type standardized, another the baseball with side mirrors, but all agreed the miner's hard hat complete with head light hard to beat. Also on the agenda were bells and horns, cops on bikes, cycle lanes and should bike couriers be licensed? Bikes on the road weren't so much an evolution to these people as a revolution. I took it all in good humor, but when 'Huperson' said, 'It gets you in touch with your feelings', enough was enough.

Anyone who has cycled any distance could tell him that the biggest feeling you get from cycling is a sore bum, and it does nothing for your libido either. Only moments before 'Huperson' spoke, I had lit up a cigarette. If looks could kill. You would think I was holding a stick of dynamite.

I left Calgary the next morning at the crack of dawn. Made Strathmore in double quick time, then left the Trans Canada Highway for Highway 21. I was now following a high ridge. Behind, I could still see the silver-topped mountains and Calgary had turned into a mid-day silhouette of sparkling gold. I was travelling in the balding foothills of Southern Alberta and every mile increased my horizon. I was making great time. My stay in Calgary had been time well spent. I felt rejuvenated. My tanks were topped. I had clean clothes and everything smelled fresh. I had oiled and greased my bike, made some minor adjustments to the pedals and taped an extra layer of foam to the saddle. Everything was A-OK until Nightingale. In thirty minutes the skies turned from blue to black, back-fired, litup, then condensed. A blast of wind later and the road was a mass of bubbling water. There seemed to be no middle ground to the weather in Alberta. Rain forced its way down my neck, stung my eyes and glued my poncho to my body. I stopped at the first farm, invited myself into their lives and was given the hayloft to bed down in.

Next morning, the farm's Maple-leaf flag hung limp. The sky was empty and the day's first light rested on the horizon. I had set my sights on leaving before sun-up, but a notice pinned to the barn door delayed me.

'DEAR BERNARD, I ENJOYED YOUR COMPANY LAST NIGHT. SORRY WE CAN'T SEE YOU OFF. YOU WILL FIND A PACKED LUNCH IN THE KITCHEN HAPPY TRAILS, CALVIN.

I'm not one for breakfasts. I like to get a good two hours under my belt before eating, but when food presents itself, I'm not one to pass it up either. On the kitchen table, I found enough food to feed an army. Home-made bread, sliced as thick as your fist and stuffed with tuna and egg salad, an orchard of apples, a couple of pears and a bunch of ripe bananas. A dozen bites later and the tuna was history. The bananas followed almost immediately, then coffee in a flask and the rest was packed away for later.

The sun was now full over the horizon and the morning stillness had blown away. A stiff breeze now bent the flag pole and, smudging the horizon, a brown streak looked on warningly. All morning the streak got bigger. Saskatchewan's top soil was on the move and, by the look of the weather, its dust storm would hit me before Drumheller.I was in a race against time. Central Alberta isn't the place to ride out storms. Bald hills don't exactly make good wind breakers and when the storm eventually struck, it swallowed me up with a vengeance. Dust, dust and more dust. Like a fine mist it found its way everywhere. It blew up my nose, down my throat and lodged in my ears. It wore me down like a soap stone. Within minutes my eyes were burnt and my skin felt like a pin cushion. I was only five kilometers from Drumheller and shelter, but I might as well have been twenty. The sun had shattered into a thou-

sand fragments, hallowed, then disappeared completely.

My descent to Drumheller was a nightmare.
Wrists and arms felt like dead weights and, to make
matters, worse my brakes were useless. I was travelling at mark speed, in control, but only just. At first,
steep banks broke the wind. Then came a switch
back. Banks shaved, opened, then pow! Instant wipe-
out. The wind hit me like a plank of wood. I was bush-
whacked. The rickshaw flipped, freed itself from my
grip, and carried me across the road like a boat under
sail. I watched the bank loom up, ploughed through its
soft-shoulder, then lost it. I was in free-fall. The sky
arched, the universe turned inside-out and I kissed the
ground.I was shattered. The bike could have snapped
in two, but I couldn't care less. I left the rickshaw on its
side, counted my wounds and spent ten minutes chasing down baggage in the wind. Miraculously, the rickshaw was intact and with the exception of a twisted
fender, paint scratches and a broken bell, totally road
worthy.

I entered Drumheller battered and bruised and
so tired, I camped at the first signs of greenery. It was
now midnight and the hushed whispers of sunset had
suddenly turned into the ghetto blasting music of
youth.

I have this golden rule about Friday nights. Stay
clear of towns. Friday nights are for the hormonally-
imbalanced. It has been like that since time began. It's
for those youths who have just crashed puberty and
don't know their ass from their elbows. It's a period we
all have to pass through. It's a time to feel your oats,
test your metal, swarm, mate and if need arise, test

their fists on each other. It certainly isn't a time to be caught out alone, tired and after dark. I have this belief that half our so-called teenage problem could be eradicated if this age group were given areas of supervision to flex their muscles. Maybe enlarged boxing rings could be refereed by 'lumber-jacks'. Having said that, I only have myself to blame for what happened that night.

I was bedded down under the roof of a barbecue pit in a small park behind the local ice rink, not exactly a secluded location. At first, my presence went unnoticed, then a scouting party, two young boys and a girl, spotted me. Reinforcements followed and soon I was the centre of nervous excitement. They were as high as kites. Drink, drugs, who knows. It doesn't take much to light the fire of confrontation when adrenalin is pumping you into a new experience. It was as if I didn't exist. They were pawing everything they saw, bike, stove, food containers. They even checked out my tobacco. They were nibbling at the inner edges of my patience and the outer edges of their courage. Slowly the chain reaction of confrontation germinated. Touch turned to twist. One of my mirrors broke. Then one word sparked it.

"Put it down."

I drew the line and they went for it. Abuse immediately turned to argument, to the threat of a fight. It was a big time stand-off. I couldn't turn tail. To pack up and leave now would only add fuel to the fire. There were girls involved. The boys had something to prove and tonight I would be their proving ground. Someone spat. I snapped, went for its owner, changed my mind mid-stream and turned on the biggest.

"Bugger off, you little prat."

Inside, I was paranoid. They were like a pack of angry wolves. You read about 'swarming' every week in Toronto newspapers. It's a term coined by the media to describe something they don't understand. There used to be a time when these rites of passage were conducted on street corners, under watchful eyes and under strict curfews that kept body and mind intact for adulthood. In today's climate, that's history. There are no watchful eyes and parental abdication is the norm, not the the exception. We have entered the era of social workers, child psychologists and one where corporal punishment is outlawed. Today's bonding rituals don't even start until midnight, stretch to the early hours and are left to the police and juvenile courtrooms for sentencing.

"Take off."

I pitched it at the leader. I was playing for time. They didn't give a damn if I was Rambo or a defenseless old maid. They were bored. I was on their patch and they wanted action. There were more than a dozen, early teens, more than a match for me. Thank God the leader backed down. I had my hand on the bicycle pump and was ready to do something stupid. They slowly turned and drained back into the shadows of the ice rink. I got the occasional curse, the half-way defiant stance, but in general,they left together like a gaggle of muttering geese. Once again, I was alone. I knew I didn't have long. Once the shock had mellowed, they'd be back. Ten minutes of back-slapping and a dare or two, that's all it would take. I didn't bother to pack. I threw everything onto the rickshaw seat, did a quick vacuum with my torch and left. I chose some bushes, tipped the rickshaw onto its side, returned to the barbecue pit for a quick look. Checked to see if there were any tell tale signs of light. No mirror reflections, no silhouettes. Everything was cloaked in darkness. I was safe.

I woke to the noise of broken glass. It was 2:00 a.m. From where I lay, I could see the barbecue pit, a flash, a crash, then another flash. Cans, bottles, and stones curved out of the darkness, passed through the light, then crashed down like motor shells.

"Wow...wow...wow...wow...wow...wow...wow."

It was the swarm. The bees were back for their honey, but the jar was empty. I had gone. A few made feeble attempts at a search, but no one stepped into the darkness for long. By 2:30 a.m. they had regrouped, lit a fire and lay back into chatter. By 4:00 a.m. the pit was deserted.

I woke at 6:00 a.m. All was clear. I did a quick inventory, packed and cycled to the nearest Donut Shop. I was still shaken up from the night's events. I ordered, visited its toilet, checked myself in the mirror, counted the extra wrinkles, put down the bags under my eyes to experience, and promised myself, 'Never on a Friday.'

From Drumheller, I turned due north on Highway 56. Cycled over a choppy sea swell of hills, then turned due east on Highway 9. I was now beginning the slow descent into the Canadian vacuum. To the south, clouded in dust and circled in birds, a solitary farmer was at work. Ducks chattered by the roadside and above a lone hawk was searching for breakfast. My first grain elevator broke through the horizon, and to the east pointing my way, telegraph poles tapered off into the late morning heat haze. I was right on schedule. Not too early to catch the biting cold winds of early spring and not too late to catch its mid summer scolding heat. Through the soft air, the sweet scent of late spring blossom came in waves. Cars were few and far between, and their exhaust didn't even register.

The days were getting noticeably longer. Wind patterns had swung from the N.E. to the S.W. and had lost much of their punch to altitude. I now wore a baseball cap more to protect my eyes as well as sun glasses, and I hadn't worn track suit bottoms since Banff. Horizons were still limited, but opening quickly. Roads were flattening out, telescoping down straight lines and, strangest of all, the billowing mountain cloud formations had stretched, snapped apart and risen thousands of feet.

I made the little hamlet of Hanna by early evening. Found an unused garage on its outskirts, made camp inside, then treated myself to a huge stew of fresh vegetables. By 7:00 pm. I was well on my way to shut-eye. I had a room with a view, a light show and a coffee to savour it with. It took thirty minutes for the sun to set. The sky smoldered. Clouds changed from bleach white to a golden orange, before firing into the deep red flames of sunset. Late evening shadows flooded the empty spaces, pooled, then were lost to an ocean of darkness. For sundowners, I drank the squeezed spice of herbal plants and the last I remember was the singing sounds of telephone wires as the wind picked up.

For once, I knew where I was heading to.

Cereal, 78 kilometers down the road, would be my next port of call. Three years before, I spent a pleasant night in its small roadside park. Back then, I was en route to Toronto from Victoria on a ten-speed bicycle. I had been a hit with the locals. 'We don't see many cyclists in these parts.' My iggly-piggly route following secondary and sometimes gravel roads through the prairies had caught many people off guard. I had completed that trip to Toronto without once having to stay in motels. I hadn't put this hospitality down to luck or cheekiness. You don't get anything for nothing in this life. A Canadian seeing Canada is unique in itself, but by bike, without a tent and off the beaten tourist routes is appreciated by all in these parts. I often felt that my presence as a house guest was payment enough. I never went without. Roadside chats were worth a chocolate bar and asking for water often led to overnight stays. People cared. They had the time and the inclination to talk and often one invite led to, 'You must visit my nephew's farm in Dolphin.' I had wanted to taste that experience again. Expose myself, not like the 'Terry Fox' look-alikes. The New Wave campaigners who cross Canada offering one minute news bites and have back-up crews as long as your arm. I wanted to go public, allow myself to be stopped, detoured and passed down the family tree. In the Rockies, I had been trapped. The Trans Canada Highway was the only logical route. It was the quickest and easiest, but I was lost to the crowd, but this time would be different.

To break up the morning's rhythm, I took a side road. The land was dry, the road graded and spirals of dust followed every car. I was only five miles away from the main road, but light years away in time. Every car slowed, waved and some stopped out of sheer curiosity. Either side smoothed fields looked like one huge farm, acres of neatly ploughed land, but no people. Only the day before the fields had been full of activity. Huge farm tractors in tank formation; some plowing, some fertilizing, a mixture that stained the air in a brown green cloud. Twenty-four hours later, I could still smell it.

I made Cereal by late afternoon. I was amazed at how many people remembered me passing through three years before, of my night under the barbecue pit, of the stories I told and of my dream to put pen to paper. It turned out to be just as good the second time around and I fell asleep with a heavy stomach.

Bernie the Bike Man
Chapter 4

News of my trip across Canada was now travelling the highways like blood through veins. Small town folk have big time networks, and requests were coming thick and fast. Last nights barbecue offered more than just food. It started with a retired teacher, an invite to visit his old school and a short detour to Oyen, and the rest was history.

I emptied the school like a sinking ship. I had just cycled into a wall of excitement. In the playground, confusion reigned supreme. Teachers were red-faced, noisy and mostly ignored. Within minutes, I was surrounded by a sea of smiling faces. My bell was rung, tassels pulled and the rickshaw's seat lost to bodies. Hands waved to attract, some to touch and others attached to pens, for autographs. For the moment, I was a star and revelled in it.

"Hello, Mr. Howgate, can you bring your rickshaw inside please?" It was the school principal. I'd touched down on his school like a typhoon, but his smile held no grudge, and like the 'Pied Piper', every one followed me inside.

"Would you like a coffee, Mr Howgate?" I had spoken to the principal only forty-five minutes earlier from a roadside tourist office, mentioned the name of the retired teacher I had met the night before, briefly described my trip across Canada, offered my services and that of the rickshaw as entertainment for the day, then proceeded to cycle into their lives.

Once inside, I was given the red carpet treatment. The principal's simple discipline had them back in their classrooms in no time and silence once again returned to the corridors. Coffee finished, I was given the guided tour.Every corner was covered, every class room visited and at noon I was officially introduced to the teachers. Being a small school, they were flexible. Time tables were rearranged, a projector found (for the slides of my previous eight year, round-the-world cycle trip that I had brought along for just such an occasion) and a school assembly inked-in. In between times the school secretary had sent my arrival down the grapevine and let gravity do the rest.

News travels fast in the prairies. Soon the phone was buzzing with inquires and by the time the students were ready to file into the gymnasium, almost every parent within striking distance was seated ready for the show.

"We have a treat for you all today." I was being introduced with all the panache one expects from a circus act. The principal was in his element. He introduced me as 'Bernie the Bike Man'. The intrepid explorer who turned his back on a lucrative life in engineering for the no-strings attached world of a travellers. He condensed my life into two minutes, then asked every one to rise, face a youthful looking thirty-something Queen Elizabeth, then swept them along through an enthusiastic'Oh Canada'.Recited the Lord's Prayer, then I was on.

I class myself first and foremost, in these situations, as an entertainer. Travel gives me a stage, and schools a captured audience to play for. I like to tease and stretch the imagination of my audience and today was no different.

"How would you like to do this?" I had them. I flashed up a picture of an Indian yogi, legs knotted behind his head. Total silence, then bursts of laughter. The next slide had them thunderstruck. African lions eating by the roadside, and the next in shock as I took them through the aftermath following a hurricane in Fiji. I was taking them on a whirlwind tour of exotic countries with hardly a pause and no sooner had one scene registered when I propelled them into the next. In quick order, I covered the Pacific, Australasia, the Indian subcontinent, ending with a spectacular eruption in Africa. For ninety minutes, I orchestrated a rock and roll concert of visual photography. Questions came from all corners, covered all age groups and were anything but boring.

"Were you ever lonely?"

"What was the purpose of your trip?"

"How much did it cost?"

"Were you ever ill?"

"What's your favourite food?"

"Did you have any girlfriends?"

I had a picture for every question and like a good comedian, I was always two steps ahead of my audience, weaving one plot into the next and leaving hooks to be bitten at every turn, in every story told.

I'd apprenticed in the art of storytelling during my round-the-world days. Visits to villages would inevitably lead to festivals and once the initial pandemonium of a school visit had subsided, I could sit for hours answering questions. Once, I was held prisoner for two days in a village in Pakistan until a translator could be found. I had earned my stripes in hundreds of villages over the years in Asia and Africa and now it was paying dividends on my own turf. I had learned the importance of animation and, whenever possible, to underline stories with facial expressions. I found children the same the whole world over; from inner city to rural; from the rarified atmosphere of the Himalayas to the sizzling humidity of equatorial Africa. Kiddies' questions cut straight to the bone and today's audience was no different. My slide show went into overtime. I was all played out and by day's end, I had payed for my supper.

That evening, I followed the school's vicar back to his house. I was to be billeted that night under his roof. We wandered down a dusty trail. He leading the way in his car, me slowly following on my rickshaw. I had time to reflect, taste the dust and smell the blossoms. It was an instant flash-back. Everywhere there were echoes of India. The wooden buildings; the curious eyes that followed me, and the makeshift village playground. Take away the cars and the satellite dishes, the surface trinkets of the good life, and nothing is much different. And as night fell and the mosquitoes needled their way under my skin, I found them just as big, just as hungry and just as furious in their appetites as their Asian counterparts.

Chapter 5
Endless Horizons

I can only imagine how it is to travel through Saskatchewan by bus. One guy who I shared a cup of coffee with in Calgary, said of this trip: 'Travelling through the Prairies is like a huge yawn, just like travelling through an open mouth'. I tried to describe the little subtleties he'd missed. The changes of roadside colour, its delicate fragrances, its dips and valleys and a sky that was forever changing. I tried to point out all those little emotions that speed over looks, but alas, they fell on deaf ears.

My first crossing by bike in 1988 left me totally exhausted. I had crossed it in a heat wave. Strange things happened at noon. The road would shimmer, move apart, then gyrate to the rhythms of passing cars. Trees would pluck apart and grain elevators change shape. Nature's hall of mirrors would have a field day. Sometimes a sea loomed up where no sea existed, then burst like a bubble. The road became a tight rope and the horizon the safety net of free-fall that never quite lived up to its promise. That was then. Today the sun's heat had been tempered by a morning rain shower. A day like today can relax body and mind just like a good whirlpool. Distances mysteriously shorten, muscles relax and you can fast forward the daily frustration of head winds, choking dust and the occasional crazy driver. At times like these, distorted shapes return to normal and eyes so used to the daily rut of objects can slide over endless horizons.

I was now passing through places like

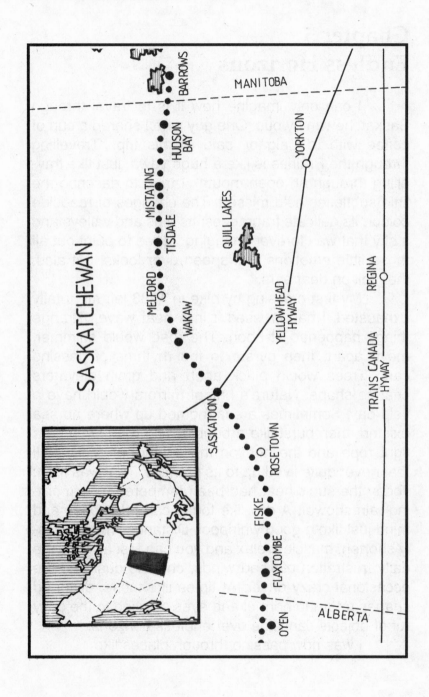

Marengo, Flaxcombe, Netherhill and D'Arcy; such names conveyed to me a sense of belonging, of continuity and hope. The quintessential New World town of waste not, want not, preferring utility constructions over extravagance and wood over stone. They were all ten-minute wonders. From entry to exit, each community I passed through all occupied the same space, all with the same ingredient of community permanence. The red-trimmed fire halls; the white wooden churches; the standard two variety stores, clothes and hardware and the inevitable hotel bar-cum-restaurant that over breakfast turned into the rumour mill of gossip. They were all patterned from the same blueprint. A main street and a nose-to-tail block of dwellings built in tight webs, more out of shelter from the extremes of climate than economy of space. These communities broke up my day, gave me a touch of human contact, and offered not only a hook to hang my daily rhythm on but the essential landmarks with their distinctive grain elevators to reel in my daily mileage.

A Prairie grain elevator stamps its mark on the surrounding countryside in the same way church spires offer the eyes of rural England restful landmarks of community occupation. 'Saskatchewan Wheat Pool' in bold red letters. The working man's chapel. They made for strong vertical statements both defying and reinforcing the flatness of the countryside they inhabited. Some people refer to them as huge phallic erections, barometers to a successful season or its failure. I notched them off like so many railway stations and no sooner had I put one behind me than another would prick the horizon in front. They were

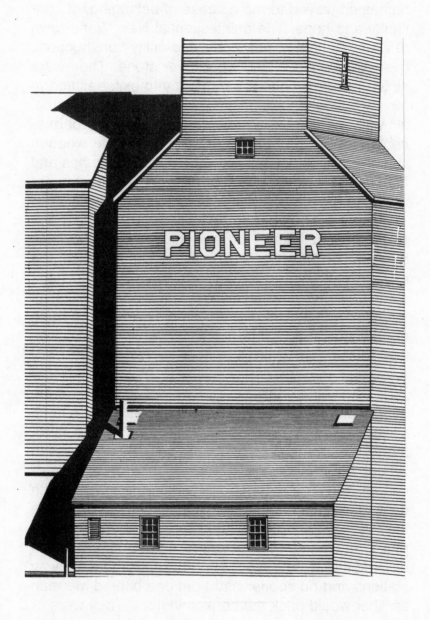

like fingers pointing the way and I found as much visual pleasure in their simple lines as in any temple.

If truth be known, I love the Prairies. They have much in common with the sea; romantic, anything but flat, with endless voids to dream in. Influences come from above and like a woman with smooth and inviting curves, its nature is slow to anger, but unforgiving if crossed. To really appreciate Saskatchewan, you have to chew well before swallowing. Patience is the name of the game. You don't buck the weather. You go when it tells you and rest at your leisure. You have to let go, be sucked in and, whatever you do, don't hold anything back.

Saskatchewan is not the sheer flat lands you read about, but gentle rolls and dips. Here the only hills rise out of steep banks, either side of rivers, as in Fiske. And in a province where time stretches to never-ending horizons, I wasn't surprised to find my days pleasantly slowing to the point of stopping.

Out in the Prairies, farms are vast, plowed-in rectangles and always topped with seed bins. Grain elevators became my mile posts and every town, a thirsty pit stop. I now found myself passing through some of the richest grain-growing farm land in the country, if not the world, but within it I found evidence to support nature's fragile balance.

Tamed by generations of farmers, its thin top soil seemed always to be in a constant state of movement. Farming, like any other occupation governed by nature's rules, could sometimes feel like skating on thin ice. No matter how fertile the soil, it still needs water and sun to work. Saskatchewan had already experienced two years of drought and was into its third. Dust storms were becoming a dangerously normal fact of life. I'd already cycled through two and it wasn't an idle joke any more when people said 'Saskatchewan's top soil was migrating west to Alberta'.

Farmers were genuinely worried. Some had already started to experiment with natural windbreakers. Bushes had been planted in rows around property lines in hope of arresting soil movement. Without wind breakers, it was like playing a game of chance where a wind storm could either strip or smother you where one farmer's misfortune could be another farmer's gain. Three dry summers and three winters with little snow had dried wells and left top soil brittle and at the mercy of the wind. Whatever rain did fall, steam dried instantly and in some areas leaves snapped to the touch. I'd not experienced morning dew since Oyen, and the lack of mosquitoes and flies was effecting everything from the bird population to the coyotes.

Most farmers had let their fields return to nature. Acres of top soil were at rest. Nature's natural carpet was allowed to take over, and yet other fields had been taken over by banks, victims of loans,mortgage rates, and over-extensions. 'Times are tough,' as one farmer put it. 'You soon find out who your friends are. It's sad to see young farmers go under, but it's natures way of weeding out the week.' I was shocked the first time I heard this, but its echo resonated everywhere. It was a case of survival of the fittest. A strange mixture of a farmer's love of the land and profit margins.

Since leaving Drumheller, I had noticed a strange lack of competitive tension in the air. Where were the prams down main street? Where were the morning school buses? School yard bike racks were empty and clothes lines barely bent under their washing loads. For sale signs littered the highways. Owner-operated family farms once bustling with children have either been converted into weekend cottages, taken-over by limited companies with their farm managers or abandoned all together. That glorious age of frontier living, its overflowing families and boundless untamed lands are history. Four generations have been put under the soil since that time and, for the stop-over visitor, its signs are all but forgotten. An old barn collapsed like a deck of cards, an over grown ice rink, a rusted out tractor, an antique Ford T and sometimes the only surface evidence that a farmhouse existed was a clump of trees. They scarred the countryside like grave stones. Some, like the family I stayed with in Fiske, had just returned from their yearly pilgrimage to visit their roots in southern Manitoba. Yesterday it was a splash of new paint, a replaced window pane and today all that remains of their parent's home is a well tended grave site. I have absolutely no idea how many people return down these same gravel roads of their youth, or what this link to the past is worth in today's society.

Guess who's coming to dinner? Unrestricted by traffic, the open roads allowed my imagination limitless opportunities to wander. Often, I pictured myself turning up at a friend's house, unannounced and completely unrecognizable, asking for a hand-out. What a gas! Today that daydream wasn't too far from the truth. I was en route to Saskatoon and my arrival was awaited. My name had been passed down the bush telegraph service of friendship. A friend of a friend and a picture of Bernie with his rickshaw, but appearances can be deceiving. The polaroid picture I speak of was taken in Calgary ten days before. I had just showered and my hair was neatly tied in a pony tail. On that occasion I had been wearing freshly laundered clothes and, to the untrained eye, looked more like your average 9 to 5 Joe than a wild eyed vagabond. I had not used a razor since Victoria and no scissor had made inroads on my hair in nine months. In fact, the last time I groomed my locks was in that same picture. It was now a shaggy mess, and my hair being of a curly nature, had knotted itself into something more akin to Rasputin than a Stephen Segal look-alike. And that was only the tip of the iceberg. The long and continual exposure to the elements had encrusted my face in a week-old foundation of dust and sweat, while white lines of strain streaked my forehead like railway crossings. I had eyes like ball bearings which had recently sunk deep into their sockets. My weight, stripped of ten pounds since the start of my trip, had lost a whopping six pounds since leaving Calgary. On a good day, I looked like death warmed-up and on a bad day, its ghostly shadow. My continuous diet of bananas, peanut butter, honey and bread had not stopped this slide. I was taking on the shape of a scaled-down bean pole with a tilt. As for my clothes, they were still hanging there, but being threadbare, only just. I was down to my last pair of socks, two 'T' shirts and my only pair of shorts had recently opened to age. I had lost a towel to a river bed, my spare runners to the darkness in Drumheller, and couldn't wait to restock at the first second-hand clothes store I came to. From a distance, I looked like a Spaghetti Western bit player, but up close, if you could fight your way through the body odour, I was a walking-cycling disaster. Through all this worry and self-discrimination, it never dawned on me that my future host in Saskatoon had gone through exactly the same thoughts. It's not that she hadn't washed in weeks, given into a starvation diet or decided that personal grooming was for the dogs. She just wasn't into appearances and thought I was. When I eventually did cross her threshold, step over her seven sitting tenants who were all cats, picked my way through her personalized furniture of garage sale leftovers and eventually found that left-over pot to boil water in, I knew I had found a kindred spirit.

It was great to lay back and pig-out with a like-minded soul, where anything goes, where dishes could be washed at your own pace and cooking done to the individual time clock of one's own appetite. In short, I had the run of the house and for the first twenty-four hours, that's just where I stayed.

Outside the weather was great and Saskatoon was bursting with colour. I gave my knee joints a rest and took up walking. I revelled in the no-nonsense people I met. The eye contact that, once made, warmed to my looks and the cheeky 'Beautiful day for walking' greetings they gave me. It was my type of place; small and compact with just the right balance of old shady neighbourhood streets, vibrant downtown core and - straddling the Saskatoon River - breezy, fly-less and dry. But after three days, I got the itch.

As much as I like these respites, the clean sheets, the multi-course menus and the bonding of friendships, I soon feel suffocated. It's not the people, it's me. There's something about the fresh air of outdoor living. The early morning slap of chill and the seduction of pastures new that makes anything more than overnight stays hard to take. So far the only exceptions had been Vancouver, Calgary and now Saskatoon. Maybe its the closeness of indoor living or the heat, all I know is, I get lazy. Not your average 9:30 a.m. fluttering eyelids of vacation blues, but your noontime bags under the eyes, mega-lazy of unemployment. When this happens, it's time to move on. I had stayed three days, tonight would be my fourth night. Any more would have been overkill.

I left Saskatoon bright and early with a tail wind for company. All sails were up and I was fair motoring. I had got into the habit of raising the passenger seat's canvas canopy on such occasions. I even found if I screwed myself up into a ball on the passenger seat, I could escape the rain. I took advantage of all the elements. The morning's stillness for those charged-up starts. The high noon heat for rests and the afternoon breezes to sail on. Any day soon the winds would change. I had been blessed with north west and south west winds since leaving Calgary, but they weren't the norm. At this time of the year, the prevailing winds should come from the east, but I'd been lucky. Many blamed this late change in the wind direction for all their ills. Last year's grass hoppers; this year's caterpillar; the freight rates; the rail strikes and the drought and dust storms. In fact, since entering Saskatchewan talk of the weather had punctured almost every sentence. Just the mere mention of a cloud, the hint of rain and all eyes would turn skywards. Only one week before in Kindersley, I had exchanged a few roadside words with 'Three Fingered Jack'.

"Where?" Jack's neck moved so quickly in the direction of my finger, I thought it would snap. I had just pointed down the road to the spot where thirty minutes earlier, I'd been dumped on.

"What did it look like?"

"What did what look like?" Jack looked at me as if I was from a different planet.

"The clouds. What did the clouds look like?"

"Black, kind of patchy with streakers." I was really getting into this conversation. After all, hadn't I spent the better part of the last ten years living out doors? Jack paused, looked a bit out of sorts, giving me that look a teacher would a pupil.

"Not bad for a beginner. What you experienced was only a trickle. I doubt if it lasted long enough to wet the top soil."

This guy was a professional climatologist. In fact, almost everyone I met since entering Saskatchewan had opinions on the subject. You didn't have to be a student of climatology to gain access to these conversations or have a copy of the 1937 Farmer's Almanac to read the writing on the wall. Drought equals dust, equals crop failure, equals bankruptcy. In fact, if it wasn't such a serious problem, these conversations would be downright hilarious. Instead of getting depressed over the daily weather forecasts they had turned them into a sport. They talked about them at breakfast, at dinner, street corners and to anyone that was interested and in Saskatchewan that meant 90% of the population. It even puts them to sleep, as in Jack's case, it's the last thing he watched before the tube is turned off. I've heard them curse it, compliment it. But god help those who get hooked on the Weather Channel's 24 hours of gloom and doom.

Who can remember the weather forecast five minutes later after your brain has been bombarded with a continual stream of analytical phrases and anxiety attacks? I mean to say, what is a Polar Alert? An A.V. Factor ? And then there is the Comfort Index! Add to all this the Hail, Blizzard and Windchill Warnings, mix in a Tornado Watch and the tasty little Mosquito Index and you have the recipe for a mega case of depression. The weather dominates their life like Mohammed does the Muslims, with Mecca being the first morning cloud to pop its head over the horizon -but today, I had other things on my mind.

It was May 9th. Tonight would be full moon and with a little luck, a clear one. The secret to nighttime cycling is to be fresh. I had catnapped for three hours under a tree near Yellow Creek and now as the sun set, my eyes opened.

In Asia I had cycled under many a full moon. In India, a different breed of animal took to the roads at night. Not able to work in the heat of the day, camels, bullock and donkeys monopolized the cool hours after sunset. They clogged up the roads, slowed down traffic and, more importantly, illuminated the night with thousands of kerosene lantern lights. Their noises didn't shock and the sound of bells hung around their necks touched areas that paled in the daylight. Canada is not Asia. I didn't expect to see camels but deer and bear weren't out of the question and, if I was lucky, a wolf or two.

I rolled up my sleeping bag and secured it with bunjis on the back seat. Anything that moved was nailed down. It wasn't the time to be careless. To losing something in this light would be lost forever. I watched till the last blush of sunset had dropped below the horizon, then just as the colours faded, the moon rose. A deep red disc blipped over the horizon, quickly at first, then as if launched into orbit, the moon started its slow arc across the night sky.

Suddenly, the night exploded with noise. Silhouettes fluttered, stopped, then started again. Bats, thousands of them, squealing as if lost, flying in jerky motion as if throwing off the day's sleep. They were up, out of the bush and gone within minutes. Then I saw a fox and I hadn't yet put foot to pedal. In the twilight everything seemed to go faster. Perceptions changed. Shadows jumped out into the road to greet me and noises startled. At first, I hoped the road would be illuminated. The moon had shed its red shield and was now whiter than white, but the road's gravel surface soaked up its illumination like a sponge. At the beginning, I had to use the corridor of bush and curb to guide me. It's a different world. Your eyes need time to focus, but when they do and you catch the rhythm of the lunar landscape, you can go all night.

Already the evening's chill had pressed out its juices and the air was thick with perfume. Above, the night sky was a blanket of stars and the moon, hanging like a disc by an invisible chord, radiated its glow in long shadows of light. To the west, I could just make out the evening glow of Saskatoon. It rested on the horizon. A faint hint of amber, like the fine mist of a far-off forest fire. Closer to home, sharp beams of light bore witness to yesterday's travel. Walkow was clearly visible. Rosthern, yesterday's alternate, and to the east, Melford rose above the dark like a mushroom of light. My eyes were still fresh but adjusting quickly. Familiar objects fell into place. A parked tractor and a far-off grain elevator. A slow moving armada of dust choked the night air, dispersed, then opened onto two beams of light. I wasn't the only one working that night. Suddenly a deer jumped into the picture and just as quickly, left. Later, I spotted a group of gazelle. From culvert to culvert, I counted only six leaps, six rainbows of motion. Later that night, I disturbed a gaggle of sleepy ducks, pissed off a flock of geese, surprised an owl eating its rodent supper roadside, and spotted another fox. The last human contact came around midnight. Passing a farm, I ignited a chorus of barking dogs. One farm dog would bark out its warning to the next and so on. It must have been the third house down the line. A beam of light illuminated my rickshaw, followed it for a few seconds, then darkness.I just had time to follow the light to its source before seeing its owner disappear behind a closed door. The world as I knew it had pulled up its shutters. I had exchanged Highway 41 for this gravel secondary road and now I owned it.

I had chosen this gravel road over the highway for one reason only. I didn't want to cause an accident.

I wasn't worried about not being seen. The rickshaw was a reflector's dream. Not only was it a needle point masterpiece of sewn-on-canvas mirrored reflectors but it had chrome that lit up like strobe lights under the moon and two dynamo-driven main beams up front and with four brilliant red tail lights, its shock value alone was at least worth nine. It looked, under the moonlit night like a cross between a mutant space craft on wheels and a land sailing ocean vessel, so God forbid that I meet someone under the influence.

After midnight my strength soared. Peaks and valleys more pronounced only one hour before started to flatten. It's times like these when you have to stay focused. Its easy to hallucinate when the bottom falls out of your head. There are not many people who can say they've seen the CN Tower from central Saskatchewan or have witnessed an orgy of shadowy bodies. Memories that night stretched to the limit. Battles turned to wars; games into championship finals, and old flames into bathing beauties. Thankfully nobody disturbed my crazy moments for had they, they surely would have taken me for a proper loony. It's hard not to give into sleep at 3:30 a.m., to just pull over, roll out the sleeping bag and fall into your dreams, but when it's all over and you experience the Prairie sunrise, its therapeutic warmth and its shower of rays, you will have accessed areas of your mind that very few people have the opportunity to touch. I had made it all the way to Melford and beyond and, when I did finally call it a day in a farmer's garage, wild horses couldn't drag me from my bed.

It is impossible to pass through Saskatchewan

without noticing the Ukrainian influence. From its vatican domed styled churches to its farmers like 'three fingered' Jack who wore their farming amputations like badges of honor, the Slavic accents and stocky build, their presence percolates through every strata of society like the rich aroma of Columbian coffee.

My first exposure to the Ukrainian psyche came in the school yard of hard knocks. My first pre-teen fight and the raw power of a ukie's punch. Then came my marriage to one, and yet another but gentler swipe. I learned at an early age about their directness, their love affair with simple things, their inbuilt antennas for the land and their hospitality.

"Come home with us for supper." The roadside question - or was it a command? - came as no surprise. But its suddenness, without any foreplay and loosely cloaked in an East European accent, was. Twenty minutes later, I was into a guided tour. It was your typical Ukrainian household; carpet, furniture and crockery were spotless and plants crowded out the sun. They grew everywhere.They hung from the ceilings, choked up the tables and seemed to grab you at every turn. Interspersed, but by no means second place to the greenery, I counted five deaths by crucifixion, three Virgin Marys and one framed black and white picture of your Holiness Pope Paul. Formalities out of the way, I was soon seated in the kitchen and up to my elbows in cut meats, cheese and bread, then the bonding started.

"Take a sip? This will put some hairs on your chest?" Well, he got it half right. The first sip singed my top lip and the second almost started a forest fire. Two hours later the walls were swaying. It was time to

leave. We had exhausted everything from politics to religion, and anyway, he had run out of his home brew. I was finishing my second cup of coffee, readying myself to go, waiting for the right opportunity when a knock on the door brought with it a fresh stock of the hard stuff. Four hours later, I was out for the count.

Chapter 6
Mosquito Country

After Tisdale it was all up hill. I was entering the green belt of bush. The Pasquia Hills' watershed was just ahead. Very shortly, I would be exchanging the refreshing breeze of open fields for the suffocating heat of shelter. Mosquitoes were now puncturing my skin at every stop and the dreaded black fly had arrived. My hair, that knotted breeding ground for lice, had become intolerable. I was scabbed from forehead to neck and my scalp, a dandruff haven of freshly laid eggs, was in a constant state of itch. A shampoo remedy would be of little help. Today's hair needed major surgery and I wouldn't have to wait long for a remedy.

"How much do you want off?"

That's not the kind of question to ask a man who looks upon haircuts with the same fear he does a tooth extraction.

"I've changed, my mind."

"Come on, stop being a baby, Bernie."

How do you you trust a complete stranger with something so precious as your hair? The last time I visited a 'stylist', the term hadn't been invented. In those days - the '60s to be precise - the term stylist meant barber and unisex salons were still places of the future. The barber shops of my youth were all male establishments, smelt more of surgical detergent than today's musk oils, gave you short back and sides whether you liked it or not, and charged you by the weight. The last time a professional touched my hair, the Roy Orbison Wave was all the rage and side-burns were still the youthful passage into the teen years. I stopped paying for hair cuts when I got married. After my divorce, I put myself in the hands of girl friends, I even took a shot at it myself once, but today the lady whose fingers plugged the scissors was not even an acquaintance. Before today, I'd never clapped eyes on her

"Don't worry, Bernie, I haven't lost one yet."

She meant her children. It was on their heads she had served her apprenticeship. I was big league material. A step up in more ways than one.

"Just lay back and enjoy it."

The cold steel was only inches from my ear. Enjoy what? I thought. Aren't those the same words a doctor tells a pregnant woman just before delivery. It was too late to turn back anyway. Her scissors were going ten to the dozen and hair was falling like snow. Suddenly a mirror appeared. A question on her part "A little more?" A plea on my part, "Well just a little." and she was back and running. I was getting lighter by the minute and for the first time in years saw my ears. Then she got personal

"Tell me, Bernie, were you ever married? Have you any children? Don't you ever get lonely? Wouldn't you rather travel with a female companion?" She was stylist and kitchen therapist rolled into one. She prodded and probed, snipped and combed. I was her captured audience and she wasn't about to let me get up until she had stripped hair and mind for all it was worth. Within fifteen minutes, I'd confessed all my sins, paid my penance in hair and been given absolution. The whirlwind ended as quickly as it started. I hardly recognized the new me and after a quick shower and shave neither did the family dog.

I stayed two days with my hairdresser's family in Mistatim. I wasn't suffering from a head cold or from aftershock. The reason for staying the extra day had nothing to do with last night's hair cut but today's rumbling belly. I had been invited to one of those uniquely rural events, 'A Pot-Luck-Supper' and my stomach craved its fix. For anyone who has never experienced one of these suppers, it falls somewhere between the New Testament's miracle of 'fishes and loaves' and a 'knees up Mother Brown' line dance. It's a mega sharing of village food washed down with toe tapping music. Tonight's venue was the school gym. Music was to be supplied by the local D.J, namely, the school principal, and the food by whomever. Nothing was written in stone. It was a case of come along, bring what you can in terms of food and money and enjoy yourself with a capital E. Tonight's Pot-Luck-Supper was in aid of a school trip. There were to be raffles, spot prizes, dancing and, of course, food.

The schedule of events started with a late afternoon walk around town. A kind of health and fitness parade of track-suit bottoms, runners and wind-breakers. Just the thing to bring on an appetite. By 6:00 p.m. the gym had been converted into a dining hall and by 6:30 p.m. all seats were taken. Tables were full to over flowing. Menu of the night included such local delicacies as moose stew, rabbit pie, cabbage rolls and the standard sweet and sour, beans and pork, potato and egg salad, and that was just for starters. It's times like these when the tortoise mentality is faster than the hare. Like a good athlete that stretches well before a race. The secret to pot-luck-suppers is endurance, nibble first, build up to a plate full by the third helping, then go for it.

Grace was said promptly at 6:45 p.m., then it was onto the serious business of eating. I tried every thing within striking distance at least once and some dishes twice. I may be only small in stature but I have a giant's appetite. I left as the music started. It was 9:00 p.m. Time to get some shut eye. The gym was rocking big time and I was in no shape to dance. I had consumed enough fuel to get me to Winnipeg and then some. I felt pregnant, not in the literal sense, but physically bursting at the seams. Food is a wonderful servant, but a terrible master. I didn't so much sleep that night, as churn, my stomach's digestive passages working overtime.

You think about the best but plan for the worst. I'd been tapering north ever since leaving the Trans Canada Highway in Alberta. I was entering the second week in June. I had expected an upturn in temperature, but the last I expected was snow. I'd not experienced morning frost since leaving the Rockies, but this morning it came back. I was actually much further north than I had planned, but not, I had thought, that much. My original route from Saskatoon was to take the Yellow Head Highway south through Yorkton to Winnipeg, but within minutes, I had changed my mind. After seven days of truck-free traffic cycling down Highway 7, the sight and sound of sixteen wheels thundering only inches from my ear was too much to take. I took a quick roadside time-out. I had no deadlines to keep. Winnipeg would still be there in July and what if I was caught out in a prairie heat wave, anything seemed better, at that moment than the sounds of industrial traffic. But today I wasn't too sure. The cycle from Hudson Bay was uncomfortably cold. Last night had been frigid and my sleeping bag welcome. The evening and morning had been mosquito free and I had woken into a fresh dawn dew crisped by a light frost. All morning the temperatures dropped. Shorts were replaced with tracksuit bottoms and a sweater recently purchased in Saskatoon now required the extra layer of insulation that a windbreaker offers. A northerly breeze gripped me like a vice and my fingers were going numb. Clouds billowed, darkened, then burst. I wouldn't have believed it unless I saw it with my own eyes. It lasted all but twenty minutes, snow, wet snow. It coated the road and settled in the trees. It can stick around for hours, days, sometimes weeks, I was told. They call it 'Spring Rain' in Saskatchewan. Thankfully the sun found its way back, and by late afternoon everything was back to normal.

I crossed the boundary between Saskatchewan and Manitoba shortly after 4:00 p.m. I had entered Barrow like an aging gun fighter. I was the new kid on the block and every pre-teen within hailing distance was bearing down with their two-wheelers. They were like pesky flies, too far away to swat, yet too close for comfort. I was being challenged at every corner. I was too tired to enter their game but the more I ignored their presence, the closer they came.

"Go home." It was the local constable to the rescue. "They are just being playful. It's not every day they get to see a bike like yours. Are you hungry?"

I could have bit his hand off. I was ravenous. It turned out that Pierre, my new host, not only acted as the local community cop, but his house acted as the local drop-in-centre and what he didn't know about local history wasn't even worth mentioning.

"Did you pass Whisky Creek?"

"Nope."

"I bet you can't guess how it got its name?"

Now there comes a time in any new relationship when you either brace yourself for the boring truth or warm to a well-invented lie and, by the look on Pierre's face, I was in for a mixture of both.

"Well it comes from drinking the devil brew." There was a slight pause. A shy sideways glance. A momentary roll of the eyes. Then with the mark of a good storyteller, he immediately trapped me in his web of humour.

"Drunken buggers, they were all drunken buggers, out to sink their brains and drown their sorrows. Back then the only work in this area was at the saw mill. In those days you worked seven days a week with time off for good behaviour. You hit the town with a vengeance. Drink and work don't mix. The saw mill's owner kept a dry mill. You could do what you wanted at the town side of the creek, but God help you if you were caught with the hard stuff at the mill side of the creek. I bet there's a fortune in antique liquor bottles under its surface".

That night Pierre's house turned into a revolving door of culture; settlers; Metis; native, they all popped their heads in to see the newcomer. They talked of reinventing the canoe, of self-reliance and of the dreaded welfare check. On the surface their outspoken thoughts sounded more like a culture put in deep freeze than any modern day alternative, but when Elija Harper's look-alike dropped in for a chat, dressed in a three-piece and holding a university degree, I knew that brushing land claims under the carpet wasn't going to be on the night's agenda.

What a can of worms. I have never been one to shy away from a good argument. I love to roll up my sleeves, opinionate until the cows come home and shoot the breeze, but tonight's discussion was definitely out of my league. To be perfectly honest, in all the years I have spent in Canada, the closest I had come to the 'native issue' were John Wayne movies and the fifties television series 'The Lone Ranger' with his side kick 'Tonto'. Until this trip, I hadn't even gotten past first base with the spoken word. Now I was talking with a First Nation's representative who not only articulated the flip-side of a life I never knew existed, but did it with passion. Government cheques - he called hush money; trapping - the southerners' view of a northern hobby farm; and hunting - the seasonal occupation that government bureaucrats viewed as sport, filled in the gaps. It was hard to get a handle on what he wanted out of life. One moment he would be blaming the government for all his ills, and the next be advocating more government money to help set up his state within a state. The only common thread, the only word that kept recurring time and time again, was 'land'. In his eyes, it was not only essential for life as he knew it, but fundamental to his wellbeing. It wasn't an exaggeration to say that, if I closed my eyes, I could almost picture him in a skull cap and beard, hunched over some ancient Jewish scroll. A downtown New York rabbi, debating the subject of Israel's biblical right to exist. Facts and figures were flying at me with the regularity of fists on a punch bag. I had thrown in the towel eons ago, but the force kept on coming. We were into the last round. What points he had made were long lost to fatigue. All I wanted was sleep. He just wouldn't, or couldn't, let go. Then he opened himself.

"We are the land of the living dead."

I reeled back like a fighter. Put all my strength into one last punch.

"From what you're saying, it would have been better for your race if we had shot you all on arrival"

That did it. I didn't mean to say we should have exterminated them. For a split second, I thought Elija had lost it. He was up off his seat in a flash. The royal 'we' finger was pointing in my direction and there was fire in his eyes.

"You got the idea, friend. Wild animals die in captivity. You should either put them down or set them free". With that, he gave me a long hard penetrating look, warmed to a smile, then left.

I woke to a sombre sky. Last night's rain beat down so hard it had been deafening. I just wanted to roll over, close my eyes and forget the bike. The sky was depressing. Clouds were dark, endless and moving south at rush hour speed. It was only a matter of time before the rain returned and I no sooner took to the road than it began to drizzle. Yesterday's freak snow storm had somehow jammed up the meteorological works. Clouds were queuing up over the Porcupine Hills and looked ready to burst. By 9:00

a.m. the drizzle had turned into a heavy patter and by half past the hour had built into a thunderous crescendo. Rain and hailstones; hailstones and rain. Whatever body heat I had gained through cycling was instantly extinguished. I was both soaked and peppered. At one point, I almost risked blindness. Hail as big as your knuckles dropped from the sky. I was just about to call it quits, pull up my canvas canopy, wrap myself in thermal foil and wait it out, when an unmistakable life sign appeared up the road. It was a plume of smoke. A snake-like whisper. The type that can only be shaped through a chimney. I grit my teeth, dug out the last of my plastic bags and headed up the road to its source.

I was stripped and changed, into my second cup of coffee and full of toasted bread and melted butter, when a place name caught my ear.

"Turn left on Highway 10. If you cycle through Mafeking, then you're going in the wrong direction."

Mafeking, now that's a name and a half. Like Kipling's 'Road to Mandalay' or those wicked stories of intrigue in 'The Raffles Hotel' in Singapore. The name Mafeking conjures up for me my first taste of pre-teen history. Of heroic struggles. The blood, steel and romance of the Boer War in South Africa. The Prairies are dotted with these little reflections. Names that have been carried thousands of miles and given new homes like Lloydminster, Aberdeen, Amsterdam, Strasbourg and Neudorf but, I digress. It was still early. Once again the sun had burnt its way through the clouds and once again I had retreated into my travel bubble of daydreams, but it didn't last long.

I was now entering what is known locally as the

'BOG'. Pierre had called it 'Mosquito Country'. 'We breed them for export in northern Manitoba. Our mosquitoes are that big they arm wrestle with you and black fly don't so much bite, as mug you'. At the time, I thought his words an idle boast, but I soon changed my mind. For two days, I had been mosquito free, now they were back with a vengeance. They returned with the sun, thirsty for blood and pissed-off big time due to the weather.

The day was turning into melted butter. In just forty eight-hours the comfort level had swung from frost to vapour. Lake Winnipegosis was boiling and humidity levels had sky rocketed. You couldn't buy a breeze for love nor money. I had to keep cycling, for to stop meant being bathed in sweat. Tree shade seduced like an oasis, but was only hallucinatory. Mosquitoes danced everywhere and black fly massed in angry clouds, ready to pounce.

By late afternoon I was a wound-up coil of crazed frustration. The mosquitoes were relentless and the black fly had taken up permanent residency in my hair line. My body felt like a chewed up pin cushion, and my mind, a bubble ready to burst. I had already donated an arm and a leg's worth of skin and blood, and by the looks of things, I'd be lucky to see sunset without donating the rest. Even if I had insect repellent, which I hadn't, they would probably lap it up. It was time for plan 'B'.

I wasn't exactly enthusiastic at the thought of caking my skin in mud, but then I didn't want to be sucked dry either. I'd learned this trick of facial mud baths in Africa. It had worked like a charm, but that was then. I doubted if North Americans were ready for my alternative medicine, but once the idea popped into my head, there was no turning back.

If only my mother could see me now. I was as happy as a pig in shit. I stopped at the first accessible slew. Ran up to it like an Olympic sprinter, then belly-flopped in with arms akimbo.

'Mud, mud glorious mud. Nothing quite like it for cooling the blood. So follow me, follow, down to the hollow, from where we shall wallow in glorious mud, mud, glorious mud........'

I could have stayed all day, but for the sound of a horn. A car stopped.

"Are you, O.K.?"

It was like being caught with your hand in the cookie jar, by a tell-tale big brother who doesn't want to join in the fun. Then it came to me. I waved my hands, twirled my fingers and gave them the universal sign for madness. If only I had a video. His mouth dropped over his chin. His eyes squinted and his hands shaded out the sun. I could only guess what went through his mind. But one thing's for sure, I made his day. He left with a smile on his face and a cheerful wave. Thirty minutes later, I wasn't so lucky. My newly-acquired Al Jolson look was a flop. I required a hose-down at Overflowing River's one and only restaurant before being served coffee.

If someone had named Overflowing River the capital of Mosquito Country, I for one would not have disagreed. That night the Manitoba vampires black-ened my mosquito net, sounded like the 'chain-saw massacre' in stereo and quiet literally stood guard all night. And, when I woke up the next morning, were still there.

As long as you look at the clock, you will get nowhere. Today, I wanted to put up some big numbers. I wanted to crash the three digit barrier, not just chip around its numbers, but shatter it. I had set my sights on reaching Wanless, 150 kilometers north and this morning anything felt possible. The day had dawned clear and perfect. I was off to a flying start. I broke camp before the mosquitoes could dust off their wings and was ten kilometers down the road before the sun rose.

Chapter 7
Have you ever seen Paris?

"What's Flin Flon like?"
"Have you ever seen Paris?"
"Yes."
"Well it's nothing like it. Will that do?"

Once we had passed through the initial fore-play, the courtesies of 'beautiful day for cycling, how are, ya'? and why Flin Flon?', I led the conversation onto more sobering subjects.

There are no easy answers to the question, 'how far?' or 'how long?' It is unfair, if not impossible to ask a person whose mode of transportation is a cocoon of glass and steel and whose nervous twitch can propel him from zero to 100 km/hr. in mere seconds to wrap his mind around the question of pedal power. It's not his fault that somewhere along the evolutionary scale, somewhere between the horse-drawn carriage and the automobile, that the pedal bicycle was skipped. Poor Bernie. Those all-important questions of time and distance, especially when asked in the middle of nowhere and requiring answers that only a fellow cyclist could understand, is something akin to that of a medieval search for the Holy Grail, so why, you may ask, do I ask these questions? Because I like challenge. It took me sometime to break this code, but when I did, it was easy.

Par example:
"How long will it take.......?"
"Two hours, boy."

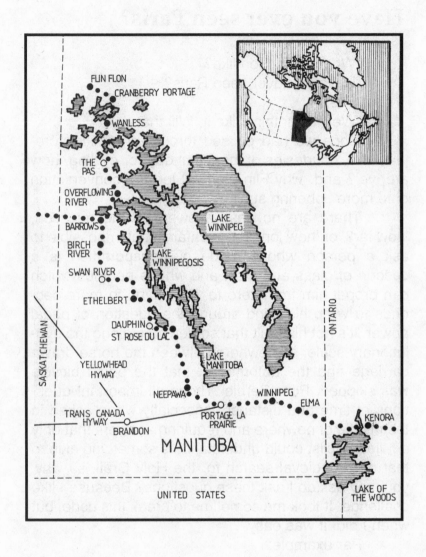

All I had to do was multiply by 10. Divide by 1.5, add the original number and round off to the nearest hour. Answer sixteen hours or one-and-a half days. And as for distance, the rule of thumb is to look to the mile posters for guidance and pray you are going in the right direction.

From Le Pas the scenery slowly changed. The straight lines and lazy curves that typified my early morning progress were now bent and twisted. Silt gave way to rock. The open reservoir of Lake Winnipegosis had narrowed to the catchment ponds of hillside drainage. I was entering a raised landscape. Air now carried with it the sweet smell of balsam and its perfumed nectar acted like a drug masking my progress. I was now entering a vast wilderness of lakes and forest. Traffic was spasmodic at best. A lone truck, a convoy of pickups and the occasional Sunday sightseer. Not exactly Yonge Street in rush hour, but I was never lonely. In these areas you still get the feeling that human contact means a lot, and if it could be gauged by the number of vehicles that either slowed out of curiosity or stopped for a chat, a very important one.

By noon, I had passed through Le Pas in overdrive.By mid afternoon, slipped into cruise control, and by early evening, I was flirting with my fuel gauge but still made Wanless with what, foolishly I thought, was plenty to spare. What a day. I had covered 150 kilometers in just over twelve hours, pushed the old machine to the limit and in the process kidded my ego that I had energy for more.

It's times like these when older heads should

prevail, but unfortunately age doesn't give one the automatic passage to wisdom. I should have taken the time to massage muscles against the onslaught of tightness. At the very least, hit the sack immediately. But no, Bernie's adrenaline was pumping and when a friendly face appeared attached to an even more inviting bottle of beer, I was all ready to celebrate.

In all my days of travel one lone physical attribute had never let me down. No matter what else failed, no matter how sick, tired or dejected I was, it just kept on ticking. In fact, it had been so reliable in the past, I thought death would overtake it. I talk of my inbuilt alarm clock. That tried and tested machine had saved me from the jaws of death during a dawn uprising in Africa; had opened to a predawn wake-up call in Asia that had propelled me to the top of a mountain for a roof top sunrise of a life time, but today it had failed me. My lids didn't even flutter. It was nearly noon before the knives of pain finally pricked my eyes open. I was racked with cramps. My neck was fused into my shoulders. My spine twisted and the soles of my feet were doing a rainbow dance. It was like morphine withdrawal and when I tried to rise, last night's indulgence just missed my sleeping bag.

I cursed, cried and pitied myself to death. Where is that partner I wanted. The one that could stroke my pain away, coo into my ear and heap all that lifesaving romantic goo that Mills and Boon swore by. Sometimes, I love self pity. I can wallow in it for hours. If only I had used my ever-faithful Tiger Balm. If only I had been nicer to that girl in Toronto back when I thought I could conquer the world. Right now, I felt

Those who think war is dangerous have not
experienced rush hour traffic in Montreal.

Coquihalla Pass, British Columbia
It took me eight hours to conquor the pass and
forty-eight hours to recover from it.

Banff National Park, British Columbia
In some places the elk outnumber the tourists.

Yoho National Park, British Columbia
Mountain Sheep are so tame they pose on request.

A secluded cove near Sheet Harbout, Nova Scotia.

Many Prairie farms once bustling with children have either been converted into weekend cottages, taken over by limited companies with farm managers or abandoned altogether.

The Big Sky country of Manitoba, you can see a storm coming long before it arrives.

I always took the secondary roads through the Praries.
A typical scene of sleepy back-road rural Alberta.

I like to travel without a tent. Meeting people is the name of the game. Last night I slept in a church, tomorrow it may be in someones house, a barn, under the stars or on a secluded beach. Tonight it was a baseball field dugout under my mosquite net.

I never leave home without my petrol stove, ample supplies of tea bags, honey and powdered milk.

My days were governed by the rise and fall of the sun,
so time zones never influenced me.

After three weeks of back-breaking days in the saddle,
I was glad to put the mountains behind me.

Rickshaws are a common sight on the Indian Subcontinent.
They have one gear and two speeds; slow and stop.

My rickshaw being assembled in Lahore, Pakistan.

There were days when I spent more time
pulling the rickshaw than peddaling it.

G.E. Barry Intermediate School, Hope, British Columbia.
My rickshaw could empty schools like a sinking ship.

Cabot Trail, Cape Breton, Nova Scotia.
Free wheeling downhill was exhilarating,
but far more stressful than pulling the rickshaw uphill.

Hoarfrost near Calgary, Alberta.

Watching a beautiful sunset is akin to a
having religious experience.

Autumn colours in Newfandland heralded the finish of my trip better than any mileage post.

Sunset over Capital Hill, Ottawa.
But no ticker-tape parade.

Nova Scotia's rugged coastline is dotted with picture-postcard
scenes like this fishing village near Halifax.

Two words sum up the character of a Maritimer
Humour and Hospitality.

Pinware River, Labrador
If you have never spent a night at sea you are missing a special treat. I spent two cozy nights storm bound on the 'Jason and Jamie'.

Saint John's, Newfoundland
Bernie at the finish line, October 29th.

Beauty and the Beast
Bernie and his Kenyan wife, Belinda in their Shamba
She likes to tell people she picked me up in a 'yard sale' ha!

conquered by it.

My breakfast stayed just the time it took to line my stomach before returning through the same orifice, and by Cranberry Portage, I had given into its vacuumed passages.

As luck would have it, the bush telegraph system of highway gossip had proceeded me. I gained an afternoon invite to the local school. I gave a thirty minute talk to its students on the wonders and pitfalls of pedal power, then thankfully sat back into the hospitality of one of its teachers. By 6:00 p.m. I was downing my first plateful of moose stew like it was my last and by 7:00 p.m. whatever lingering stress stuck to my skin was showered away. And after ten glorious hours of sleep between clean sheets, I was ready once more to greet the world.

Another day, another page. I couldn't wait to attack the hills. Once again the scenery changed. The rocks were steeper, bigger and were soon jumping out like strip posters of psychedelic colour.

UP YOURS
GRAD 71
SEAN LOVES JULIE

Every rock formation within reach carried a message. Sexual practices were advertised, loved ones announced. 'Sex, Drugs and Rock and Roll' vied with 'Jesus Loves U' and even Brian's holy name came under attack. Whoever said roadside graffiti spoils the environment should be put down immediately as a boring old fart. Free and democratic, these roadside billboards were like pieces of a jigsaw puzzle and read better than any guide book to the regions character. Raunchy styles left little to the imagination. Some of these art forms were amazing, but didn't quite have the pedigree to get into a gallery. They were always welcome and, more often than not, broke up the monotony of the open road.

I couldn't have planned my arrival in Flin Flon any better. Not only had I arrived mid afternoon, the quietest time of the day, but I found its Tourist Office had already been prewarned of my arrival.To understand the importance which I attach to these offices, I would have to remind the reader of the fundamental reason I travel. 'TO MEET PEOPLE'. Small towns have huge hearts and if you are willing to drop your defences, offer yourself up freely, 'your cup' as the saying goes, 'will runneth over'. I need their local internet of gossip to get the message out that 'Bernie's in Town'.

"What schools have you got in Flin Flon?" By the expression on the young girl's face at the other side of the counter, my question wasn't exactly what her employers had briefed her about. To be fair, I don't exactly look like your average tourist, and the type of questions I asked don't exactly fall within the tourist office's terms of reference. But I just seem to have this inbuilt gift of getting what I want. Like a good striptease artist that can pull your string without making contact, I have the gift of being able to charm, disarm and transport people into my picture without them even knowing. Of course, it helps to have a colourful rickshaw parked outside and an impish smile, but then, I never said I was God.

Within minutes my arrival was being telephoned from one school to the next.

"We have a world traveller in our office. He's cycled all the way from Vancouver. He says he's willing to give a free slide show and talk on his travels at your school if one of your teachers can put him up for the night". The bait was out. My stay, whether it was going to be a one-night stand under the stars or a night of fun and games with local characters, was now out of my hands. All I could do was sit back and wait.

"I've had a word with the principal of Hapnot Collegiate. Just go to the reception and ask for Gerry." It was as easy as that. Here I was, only sixty minutes in Flin Flon, cycling down a road I had never cycled on before, heading for an appointment with a person I'd never seen before. It was like a blind date, but a blind date with a twist. I mean to say, who in their right mind is going to invite someone into his home, expose wife and children, not to mention a classroom of his students, to a talk on subjects he may not be too comfortable with by a complete stranger. Who else, but another kindred spirit.

What makes big men shy and small men aggressive? Who cares. What a match we made. Gerry and Bernie. Bubble and Squeak. Batman and Robin. Gerry, the tall subdued volcano with a current of seriousness, and Moi; short, bubbly and the selfappointed opinionater of the universe. From the word go, Bernie was a happy camper and before the day was finished, I had been swept along by Gerry's warmhearted nature from school to his wife Linda's kitchen and beyond. I slipped into their lives like an old glove. I had entered a household of organized disorder. Just another mouth to feed and to argue with over the TV's remote control ownership. The free-spirited bachelor and the radical-minded father. Two people poles apart on the surface, yet united in a single belief of sharing. That I could stay longer than one night was never in question. How I could leave without staining my cheeks was another. Hello and goodbye; hasta la vista, the stronger the root, the deeper the cut. I ended up staying six glorious days. I revelled in the cut and parry of regular life and, within its four walls of normality, was totally at peace.

'The grass is always greener', so the saying goes, 'on the other side'. I've always been a misplaced traveller with cravings for stability and Gerry turned into my alter ego. For five days, he shared his family with me. He was the calm in the eye of the hurricane. The dreamer who sits back, lost in the crowd but always noticed. Too many sentences have been written and too many images sold in the pursuit of adventure when the greatest adventure is family life itself. I can't speak for women, but I know that many men envy my life style. The universal freewheeler. A girl in every port. If only they knew. A root transplanted can be stumped at birth. Stability, constant care and food are their staple diets. I am just a side show. A dream machine for the masses. A root in constant motion. 'But for the grace of God, go I'. For six days, I lived the life of normality. Just one of the boys. Just another Joe who could pick his nose with the best of them, fart up a storm after a plateful of beans, but most of all, just be himself. This experience, this injection of normality hadn't been the first on my trip and no doubt wouldn't be my last. But when I eventually turned tail and headed south back down Highway 10, I knew it had been special. A male bonding par excellence and something I knew would pass the test of time.

Chapter 8
Summer at Last

It was now mid June. The time spent in Flin Flon had put summer on hold. I had retraced my steps down Highway 10 through the 'Bog' and seen no difference, but no sooner had I turned onto Route 269 at Ethelbert than I noticed summer had overtaken me. It was an amazing change, like turning a page. Fields had turned from seedlings to waist-deep shoots. Here, I was less impressed by the power of nature than its fertility. Sun flower seeds that take root in May and grow at the rate of an inch per day until the end of their cycle in July. A bank of soil, piled by a bulldozer, that clothes itself in a single season in ferns and rushes, and the lovely flowers of jewel weed hanging higher than your head. It was summer at last. Today a colourful striped carpet, like a staircase flattened and laid to rest on either side of the road, corridored my progress and echoed everywhere to the sounds of insects. Bees were working overtime. The winged agents of fertility were spawning every flower in sight. It was much different from the fragile ecology of the Plains with their rawhide-smooth hills. Here, under the influence of Riding Mountain to the west and Lake Dauphin to the east, everything was in abundance. Nature had a strangle hold and everything left unkempt returned back to it, sooner rather than later.

The route from Mafeking to Dauphin was a strange mix of contradictions. The land looked so fertile, so strongly rooted, that its wild nature bore all the signs of suffocating its guardians. Just as in

Saskatchewan, the small farmer had been evicted through the combined forces of nature and global economy to seek tamer pastures. Paths leading nowhere, barns half collapsed and some barely recognizable, half submerged like sinking battleships, marked the sight as clearly as grave stones at deceased homesteads. I passed at least two impressive Ukrainian churches, both wood, dried and fried by

years of neglect, paint peeled and stripped like weeping tears of congregations long since gone. I had passed one village after the next, disease ridden, bloated and rotting, yet still life clung on. New more economical homes were sprouting up. Smaller, more utilitarian and every now and then a newly erected sign, freshly painted, shouted out roadside, demanding to be read. Satellite dishes like sails in the wind bore evidence to newer technologies and young children sitting astride mini four-wheeled UV's to an age of expensive toys.

Since leaving Flin Flon, I had been blessed with glorious weather. I had camped out overnight under the stars. At Birch river, I built a roaring fire down by its banks, then lost myself mesmerized by its sparks and embers. In Ethbert, I was seduced by the smell of a young family's barbecue and after eating my fill, lay back into the sight and sound of an early evening baseball game, before turning its empty diamond into my bed. For four days the skies had been clear and it wasn't until I reached the semi-plains of Dauphin that its picture filled in.

It is true, what they say, that the prairie horizon can be overpowering. Its slow moving, seemingly endless landscape soaks up one's concentration like a sponge. In a car this section of Canada can be an ordeal at the best of times, but for a cyclist, exposed to the elements, under an ever-changing sky, it's a different story.

Every day the sky would fill up with collages, an ever-changing, mind-spinning array of images that within minutes settle on the brain with meaning and shape, then just as suddenly vanish. These images are powerful, more compelling than canvasses, and impossible to capture in a single frame. They can be the messengers of feast or famine, either intimidate or calm. They have a unique power and a code that, once broken, read like an hourly weather bulletin.

By now, I had become quite an expert at reading their formations. Billowing clouds meant windless days. Angular patterns denoted weather fronts and when smudged, made for windy days. Overlapping low and high pressure patterns, linked, squeezed and eventually emptied cloud formations like punctured balloons with dark vertical traces bearing evidence to their rainfall. I was always on the leading edge of change. My head tilted with one eye on the road and the other sky bound, and it tested my knowledge at every turn.

In Dauphin, I stopped to top up on peanut butter and honey, and in the process, became the recipient of an impromptu lesson in weather forecasting.

"Let me show you how to read the weather."

I'd struck up a conversation with an old farmer and he was now about to show me how to read the clouds. He started by prodding and waving his index finger like a baton in the sky. A crow was hovering motionless above us. For some moments he watched it, then breathing deeply through his nose, he proceeded to smell and taste imaginary measures of air, like a wine connoisseur, before offering his weather forecast.

"It's gonna be a chilly day. Wind al'be out'a north east. Could be a storm brewing."

I was amazed. "How do you do this?" I asked.

The old man's expression warmed. His eyes were dancing and the deep routed lines around his cheeks snapped back like elastic bands. He could hardly restrain his answer.

"Saw it on the Weather Channel."

Was nothing sacred? Another illusion shattered, but what a good lesson.

Today I was only six kilometers from Neepawa

and shelter. Above, the clouds were moving big time. Clouds mushroomed like germs under heat. Up till now, I'd been lucky. I had skirted several storms in Saskatchewan and yesterday spotted one brewing on the horizon, but today my luck ran out. I was on a collision course and to make matters worse, a snake-like tail danced menacingly under the blackest cloud.

I was cycling in a purple patch. It was the calm before the storm. The air was still. The atmosphere charged and the sky empty of birds. Distant lightning flashed like strobe lights. A vertical streak. A zig-zag of pulsating light and ripples of thunder. On either side dark curtains fell in gauntlets of rain, then the storm struck. I was side-swiped. A sudden blast of wind. sandblasted and blinded all in the same moment. The rickshaw took on a life of its own. Its canopy ballooned. We ran with the wind. I was taken from one side of the road to the other, tipped, then bucked off. The rickshaw capsized, skidded on its side, righted itself down a gully then was lost from sight. By now all signs of the sun were eclipsed. Lightning flashed, bounced then cracked in my ears like a depth charge. Zac..Zac..Zac.....Pow..!   Zac..Zac..Zac...Pow..! Then the hail struck. Freeze-dried chunks, some as big as golf balls. Within minutes the road was glazed in ice pellets. They bounced rolled and kissed each other. They stung my head, nipped my neck and cracked my knuckles. It was awesome. Light blue balls of ice against a pitch black sky. For five minutes they literally poured down. The Prairies, I had been told, don't do anything in miniature and today was no exception. The Plains Indians took the appearance of these storms as dire warning. The prelude of fire, floods and plagues. It sounds almost biblical by today's standards. The nineties generation are the children of technology. We live in an age that has been blunted by science and cushioned by insurance companies. Natural wonders are for the 'Discovery Channel' or the Claims Brokers' but to be centred in one, to be alone, to be past the point of fear, is to be exhilarated and deflated all in the same breath. I swore I saw lightning bounce only yards away. I saw its steam pattern rise, smelt the burning tar from the road. I held ice pellets as big as knuckles, tasted and squeezed them so tight it numbed my fingers. It was one of those experiences money can't buy. Had it struck ten minutes later; had I found shelter, felt less exposed or been able to shared the experience, I might be writing a different story.

Thirty minutes later peace returned. The sun burst out again scattering the clouds. Steam rose, vaporized and stained the air with the sweet smell of wheat. Soon the sky was bleached white, and not long after the road steam dried. Almost everything bore witness to the storm. Fields flattened, low points lost to lakes and grain sheds upturned. Neepewa hadn't escaped either. Some trees had been uprooted and rested on their neighbours. Branches snapped like match sticks, lay in the road, and pavements were lost to leaves. In a strange way this natural experience opened the door to one of a more human variety.

Sometimes you need an outside jolt to put life into perspective. All too often my thoughts and actions during my trips revolve around my own needs. I become selfish. It's only natural. People come and go like a revolving door. Some make lasting impressions, but most never reach the filing tray. I am normally attracted to the radical outsider. The individual who swims against the currents of convention, but today's wheels were pointing in the direction of a different radical, the tried and tested collective type of communal faith. I am no stranger to closed societies. I once gave in to a Christian cult, but couldn't live with its 'praise the lords'. I have also experienced the hippy life of free love, but couldn't keep up with my partners, and I have dipped my toes into the New Age, inner city communal life of shared accommodation, but couldn't stand the freeriders of life it often spawned. I am just made from a different mold. Too selfish, I suppose. But still, these groups intrigue me. There is just something about people who can yield themselves absolutely to a faith. Who can exchange life's excitement, its menus of highs and lows for the table of contentment. Of course, it helps if you are born into it and I think there, for me, lies the attraction. The virginal quality of the unspoiled. The naive childlike security of tunnel vision.

I had been told that just outside town I could find a Hutterite colony. I knew of Mennonites, but as for Hutterites, all I knew is what I had seen and outside their dress code - a cross between turn-of-the-century Quaker simplicity with the long plaid checked skirts of their women and the Lincon look-alikes of their men with their statesman-like black overcoats, braced trousers and square chinned beards - I knew nothing. And if I had learned anything from life, it's that appearances, especially of the unusual variety, can isolate a person or a group of people as effectively as fenced-in boundaries.

Fifty years ago, before the advent of television

and its message of universal cloning, I am positive these colonies not only flourished but blended into the landscape like a patchwork quilt. I am sure they would have been treated with the same respect and distance one neighbour treats another. This isolated mentality allowed the cultural backwaters to exist, but the Canadian birth geography has changed much in the intervening years. It is common knowledge that at one time rural Canada exported its surplus to the cities. Now the tide is in the opposite direction and with it, a new set of values. People are more self-centred. I am the biggest exponent of the me, me, me, generation, I know. I have always looked upon the Hutterites and colonies like them as the custodians of old family values. The patriarchal system that teaches men to be self-reliant and women to be supportive has always attracted me and the more I thought about them, the more I wanted to enter their time machine and go back.

Turning my wheels into their courtyard, the only thing I could think of was my nicotine-stained fingers and my shorts, worn and tattered that barely protected my sex. I was self conscious from the tips of my toes to the top of my head.

News of the stranger's arrival spread like wild fire. Within minutes, I was completely circled by a throng of excited children. Then it was the women's turn. Shy at first. They played with me from a distance. Eyes followed my every gesture. Their giggles hidden by cupped hands were music to my ears. I was being undressed without a hint of sex. They pried, teased and bared my emotions. The scene was following the same pattern I had experienced on numerous occasions in the remote villages of Asia and Africa. They were applying a litmus test and when a youth stepped forward and introduced himself, I knew I had reached the first rung of the ladder. I now began to slowly climb up the ritual pecking order, ending up almost one hour later at the doorstep of the colony's spiritual leader.

"Come in. Welcome. God bless you."

From doorstep to kitchen the old man never once released his grip of my hand.

"Please, take a seat. My wife will bring you a bowl of stew."

The old man was built like a brick shit-house. Solid as a rock, short and squat with a grip as firm and determined as his chiselled chin looked. There was an elf-like quality of mischievousness in his eyes and when his wife appeared, they almost looked like identical twins. Both were cast from the same mold, one to swing an axe and the other to bear children. Both jobs of equal value, and by their shape and size, both requiring equal portions of strength and endurance.

I was now under mother's care. Fresh fruit filled the table. Homemade bread, butter and cheese quickly followed, and before the main course of home-made beef stew appeared, I was already two-thirds full.

Looking back at my stay, it's hard to pick out one highlight. There was the excitement of my initial entrance. The first time I allowed a child to sit astride my bike and the sight of it disappearing behind a barn wall being chased by half a dozen antique miniature look-alikes. Then there was my introduction to the communal kitchen. The smell of freshly made bread and the creamy texture of their unpasteurized milk, which lingered for hours. I will always cherish the school visit I made; remember the two pre-adolescent boys whose female counterparts teased them unmercilessly. I carry with me until this day the background hum of chatter, and the squeals of joy. The tears and the unrestrained spontaneity of their emotions. Everything with the exception of their new computerized dairy feeder had that worn-in look. They all had character with a capital C. I had expected a boring uniformity, but found they had room for more. They had made adjustments, interpretations and I had found them human. When I finally left it wasn't the details I carried away with me, but the sum total of their collective parts. Their credo that read 'be honest with yourself'. They were all characters. All reflections of the whole, yet individuals in their own right. I was glad I had made the effort to detour. I gave in to the experience, felt a better person for it, but knew I wouldn't return.

Chapter 9
All good things come to an end

It was hotter than hell and as flat as a pancake. The wind cut through to the bone and the sun barbecued my skin. Today would be my last day of prairie cycling. I had set my sights on Winnipeg by nightfall and I just wanted to spend the day in reflection.

In the city your eyes are landscaped for you. Grass is manicured, trees planted for aesthetics and manmade waterways travel by design. I was going to miss the prairie landscape. Its blood red sunsets and its many layered sunrises of colour. I was going to miss all those hawks and owls that watched over my progress and all the phallic-shaped granaries that beaconed my way. Where else but on the Prairies can you see wild chickens in abundance, spot early morning deer grazing roadside and enjoy daily pit stops in postage stamps of rural business called towns? Who in their right mind could not give in to the seduction of their local 'five and dime' department stores, warm to their 'beautiful day' greetings and be assured of personalized service?There is something compelling about this lack of vulgarity. Billboards are almost non existent and neon signs something of the future. With few distractions, life is simplicity itself. I had met and befriended people of limited diction, whose vocabulary illustrated through a language of expression would be the envy of most deaf people. I had laughed and joked with complete strangers and was welcomed as a breath of fresh air at every turn. If it sounds like a superior culture, then maybe it is. When God calls me, I hope I can talk him out of it, but if I can't and I had one last wish, I would like to return to the plains, experience one last silver dish of full moon, sleep under its blanket of stars and trace its milky way into infinity.

All good things have to come to an end sooner or later, but I didn't think it was going to end so abruptly. My first full day in Winnipeg and the honeymoon was over. I had expected a morally neater place, but in stead entered a colourful world of hookers, drunks and panhandlers. This was the province where Canadian medicare had been conceived, where the co-operative movement took root. That neat little picture I'd carried based on conversations only proved to me how little you can learn without firsthand experience, but one thing hadn't changed."Goddam wind," said the man. "If it ever stops blowing, we'd all fall flat on our faces." I had made a pilgrimage to Portage and Main. I wanted to test out that Manitoba boast about its intersection being the windiest in North America.

My stay in Winnipeg was punctuated between making new friends, taping fifteen-second news bites for the local TV stations and making much needed repairs to my rickshaw. The stress of 2500 kilometers had taken its toll. My pedals needed an overhaul. My padded saddle had recently split and required a saw job, but the most worrisome detail was my chain; it had stretched. The last week, I had been on and off the saddle like a yo-yo. The chain slipped at the slightest bump. I had already taken one chain link out in Calgary but that seemed to only add to the problem. I put the message out that I wanted a heavy duty chain,

I even mentioned it in my interview and I had just about given up hope when I spotted a cyclist in town sitting astride an antique single-speed bicycle. I chased him down, explained my problem and by day's end, I had a new chain; free gratis, care of a bicycle repair shop. Bike repairs over, I fell into an orgy of writing. I hadn't touched base with friends in over two months. I was closing in fast on the half-way mark and I wanted to share my enthusiasm. The rickshaw cycled as good as new and I felt fitter and looked younger than in years. I was crashing the 100 km/day barrier on a regular basis and the thought of reaching Newfoundland before the onset of winter, seemed more a reality than a dream. I stayed a full week. Spent most of my time in bed and when it came time to leave, was as fresh as a daisy.

That evening, I made Elma. The last stop on the CN Railway line before it crossed into Ontario. From there, I headed south on Route 11 before rejoining the Trans Canada Highway for the long 700 kilometre haul to Thunder Bay.

Chapter 10
The long green tunnel

Slowly my horizons shortened. Trees now bridged the road. I was entering the long green tunnel of Ontario's northern wilderness. After weeks of expanded horizons, unrestricted air movement and blazing colours this new repetition of trees, rocks and shade was almost claustrophobic. The sum of these parts plus the increased volume of traffic drained my enthusiasm like a leaky cup. And when the black fly struck up a hungry acquaintance with the back of my neck, I got downright depressed. So, I was in no mood for the argument that followed.

Kenora has more NativeIndians than you can shake a stick at, and they get it shaken at them quite often I had been told. So it came as a pleasant surprise that one of their brethren would come that evening to my rescue. It started innocently enough. I had pulled into a picnic spot down by the shore of Lake of the Woods. I had unrolled my thermal mat, erected my protective mosquito net and was half way through preparing my evening meal when an over-zealous park warden descended on me.

To set the scene, I should first advise the reader that Bernie's from the old school. An old-fashioned chauvinist in the true sense of the word. There are certain laws like gravity you don't tamper with and one is you never ever strike a woman. As a youth, still under the protective wing of my mother, just the mere hint of

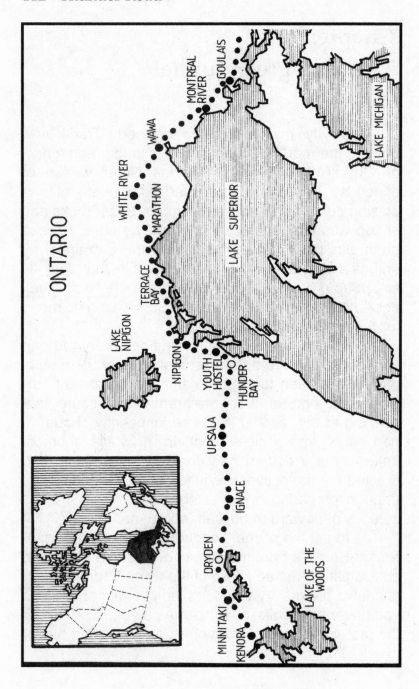

a pre-emotive strike against her was worth ten minutes in the sin-bin, and a raised hand, even through self defence, meant I was gone for the night. My mother possessed a wicked right hand, but tempered its force with a velvet glove and never abused her status as 'Lady of the Manor'. With this in mind, imagine my total lack of defence against a female park warden when the verbal abuse started.

"What are you doing here? It's against the law to stay overnight. I want you packed up and out of the park in ten minutes or I will call the police."

What is it about uniforms that make boys feel like men and women feel they are in a permanent state of menopause? In two minutes flat this lady had reduced me to a quivering jelly fish. I felt like she had kicked me in the balls and was now threading my third testicle. She was hovering around me like a hungry vulture. A prod here. A prod there. She was relentless. Then it happened. She was half way through her third, "Get a move on" when she just stopped in her tracks.

"Leave the fukka alone." A toothless grin came to my rescue. If you haven't ever witnessed a cock fight, I can tell you it's not a pretty sight. They set about each other with total abandon. The air turned blue. In one corner, my self-appointed champion was a middle-aged Indian with even a bigger middle-age belly and in the other corner, shirt sleeves folded up to her ample biceps, was my female protagonist. It was a match made in heaven. They didn't even shadow box. It was down and dirty from the first bell. After five minutes of non-stop action they called it a draw. My newfound friend looked exhausted, while the lady warden, plumage all a-flutter, bore all the signs of tension relief.

It wasn't that I felt I owed him one for championing my defence, that I followed him. In fact, I do believe he had enjoyed every moment, 'Good entertainment' as he put it. I was just too tired to go it alone that night. We made an odd match. He hadn't a care in the world. He never once answered my queries. 'How far?' or 'Where are you taking me?' I was tired, hungry and still a little shaken from the incident with the park warden. To him, I was a catch. The tourist who had just been blasted by a park warden and a female one at that. As it turned out, we were heading in the direction of the local reserve. Every now and then someone would appear, give me a sheepish grin, laugh at my friend's story, then quietly fall into step. No one was in a hurry. We did the rounds. 'This is where my father lives. My uncle. My brother. My step-brother'. I lost count of his relatives. It seemed the whole village had some blood running through his veins We eventually wound our way back down to the lake. He left me just before sunset at the reserve's Community Centre. I set up camp under its veranda, watched the moon rise and eventually fell asleep to the overlapping sounds of children playing and dogs howling.

Like a dimmer switch in a cinema, Kenora's early morning rays shut down with the clouds. Birds quietened, winds stilled and the temperature dropped. A thick screen of mosquitoes went on a drinking binge, but disappeared with the rain. It started like a fine mist, turned into light pellets and ended in a glazed sheet that stung my eyes. I was now cycling tight up against the side of the road. What protective shoulder the

Trans Canada Highway offered had disappeared on leaving Kenora. I was now forced to leave the road for approaching traffic, not just any traffic, but your sixteen-wheeler kind of traffic.

There may be, in the dusty old archives of Toronto's Royal Canadian Yacht Club, an old sea code that requires ships to give way to sailboats, but I have yet to hear of a similar code that requires motorized vehicles to give way to the bike. It's just not feasible, no matter how well-intentioned the arguments bannered by the cycling lobbiest. I've always worked on the principle of survival of the fittest. If you haven't got the power, then you finesse it and, for me, that meant riding the hard shoulder's white line like a tight rope walker and embracing its soft shoulder whenever a sixteen- wheeler approached. There is a golden rule which applies on the Trans Canada Highway, especially on the section between Kenora and Thunder Bay which has little to zero hard shoulder to boast of, and that is; everything gives way to trucks; cars give way to buses and bikes to all the above mentioned. Visibility, that is my secret. It's no good cursing a side-swipe, a brush-off or a roadside shower. Almost all drivers had ridden a bicycle in the past or have children who do. It's no good shaking your fist, cursing or using intimidatory tactics like hogging the road. If you have a mind set that motorized vehicles are your enemy, they will just wear you down. Accidents do happen. You can't make allowances for the psychopath or the drunk, but you can cut the odds down by being cautious, courteous and diplomatic. Once your presence has been noticed by the truckies (they can be your worst enemy or your best friend) and your 'handle' has hit their C.B. airwaves, 'Watch out for that crazy three-wheeler. I saw him a few miles back down the road. Do you copy? Over,' you are home and dry.

As evening approached the sky cleared. The air filled with the perfume of balsam and spruce. Birds gathered for their nightly coupling rituals of song and the bronze glow of sunset lit up the western sky. I wasn't in a panic. My dynamo-powered lights lit up the rickshaw like a Christmas tree and Dryden was just around the corner. I was heading for one of those rare shelters you don't find mentioned in guide books and to give its location away to the uninitiated would be to lay it open to abuse.

Under Canada's hard northern shield lies an underbelly of amazing warmth and hospitality. The inner city may have cornered the market in shelters for the homeless, but its rural setting-churches with doors left unlocked, ruled only by the 'honour system'-have been, since Christendom, the custodians of shelter for the tired and weary traveller. Don't ask me how I can spot them. They have always been there when I have needed them. Sometimes a short courtesy call to a neighbourhood house is in order, but usually all I've had to do is pull up, open its doors, sign the guest book, then relax. Sometimes you can find a collapsible bed in the rectory. Sometimes even a note (telephone number) which invariably leads to a night between clean sheets at the parsonage, but normally sleeping arrangements are optional. I have slept in Catholic churches, Baptist, Lutheran, Protestant with Evangelical orders and even in a Sikh Temple. Nine times out of ten you will be spotted on entry and with the payment of exchanged stories, food invariably follows.

I found this church by accident. Three years before, I was on the final leg of a round-the-world bicycle trip en route to Toronto. It was getting dark. I carried no tent and, like today, it had rained all day. I had just passed the church and was speeding towards Dryden's lights when I had a puncture. Now, I am back again.

Who said life is a carousel? I had just spent a peaceful night camped by the side of a church altar, woken to a beautiful sunset, eaten breakfast served by a lady whose voice gave new meaning to the phrase 'have a nice day', then proceeded to cycle into a minefield of road construction.

The Trans Canada Highway is always under

repair, but so far I'd been lucky. Construction in the north isn't the localized patchwork job where the traveller can take alternative routes. In these parts they're mega projects and go on forever. Roads slip and slide in the rain and choke with dust in the heat. Pot holes are craters and detours turn into expeditions. I even heard rumours of people starving to death waiting for the 'green light' to go, but these were rumours. Overnight industries feed on its casualties and in one season, garage owners in the right location can make a fortune. On some of the more prestigious road constructions, government ministers have penned their names, but on others, wiser heads have prevailed.

I had no sooner left the smoke-stack-stained sky of Dryden's work horse pulp mill behind me when I ran afoul of this road construction. The bike's wash and blow-dry from yesterday's rain was soon lost to an inch thick coating of dust and dirt and peddling now sounded more like a grinder's wheel than a well-oiled machine. I found myself cycling more distance rounding craters in the road than going forward. My water bottle was empty and what drinkable water I did see, lay tantalizingly on the wrong side of bogs or down rocky clefts. When trucks passed, the sun eclipsed and cars showered me with pebbles. It was like a bad dream, and if that wasn't enough, my hopes would soar when I hit pavement only to shatter like the road back into construction one kilometer later.

At last, somewhere between Borups Corner and Ignace, the construction ended. The blanket of dust that had obstructed the road now gave way to bursts of colour and, with it, another headache.

Nature's answer to the sperm bank was in

flight. Bees, millions of them. They bounced off my head, crawled up my legs, got lost down my T-shirt and one stung me. Placid by nature, they fly from A to B in straight lines, but why their hives always seem to be on the wrong side of the road, God only knows. And if it wasn't them, it was the dreaded hornet. My calendar of information told me that the black fly season should have been nearly over, but they didn't seem to know it and last night's rain had hatched another batch of thirsty mosquitoes. All in all, it was just one of those days better forgotten than remembered, but then it only takes one incident to make a day, and when I sat down for a coffee break, dislodged what I thought to be fungi, only to be attacked by a swarm of pesky yellow-stripes, the day was duly logged, itemized and filed away.

I made Thunder Bay in a trance-like state. The road had flattened and traffic thinned to a trickle. It was the end of June, almost mid-summer in the north, but the temperatures had plummeted. I had expected early morning frost in Dryden. A hint of ice in Ignace and now the winds had swung around from the north east, a sure sign that bad weather was on the way. I was now cycling through vast tracts of wilderness. The infinite choice of prairie campsites were a thing of the past. The pressure had been on to reach Ignace by nightfall and the decision to continue past English River to Upsala nearly turned into my last. Fog, as thick as pea soup came from nowhere. Twice I had to leave the road, or become just another accident statistic. Even with my lights on, I was becoming a lethal obstruction, an accident waiting to happen, and the last time I left the road because of oncoming traffic, I ended up in a bog.

I was now in the middle of my trip, far from home and its friendly encouragement. More and more as the nights fell, my mind would drift back home. I would picture a local bar. A night out with the boys. Homemade meals and a warm body to lay with. Everything was better than my damp sleeping bag. I was experiencing a rush of fever. Sexual fantasies in the saddle have a price and for me it's loneliness. Every trip has its low points and today I had dipped under its threshold. I was depressed as hell.

I was still cold and wet. The pre-morning lining of red haze had just appeared on the horizon and above, the clouds had emptied themselves from the sky. I tried my best to salvage and repack what dry clothes I had left, then picking my way through knee deep puddles of mud, I made my way towards the only light around in Upsala. Eight hours before I had debated whether to shelter there, but its noises kept me away. It still looked the same, but its parking lot of sixteen wheelers had long since gone.The truck stop looked deserted, but its illuminated 24-hour sign held out a promise of hot coffee that I couldn't refuse.

When I meet a beautiful girl, I always react quickly. My mind can race onto level two, but my body is still under hormonal attack and this invariably leads to mistakes. Her looks had the quality that went straight between your legs. I mean she got your attention in a hurry.

"Where did you come from?" Behind sunglasses her eyes were deadened. The lines from her thin lipped mouth creased her face at sharp angry angles and her dark hair hung over her shoulders like a million strip metal cuttings. She looked out of my league, but then I didn't make the first move.

"Want to know how I got here?" It turned out she was a body for hire waiting for a lift and was looking for conversation to fill in the time. Strange as it sounds, we had many things in common. We both wanted more from life than was normal and we both had been burned. Her passport out had been a bus ticket and in her own words she had 'struck gold' in Thunder Bay, or to be more precise her body had. We had both blurred the lines between good and evil to earn a living and we both relied on our bodies to get us where we were going. We sat over coffee exchanging notes. Her slit-eyed view of life's darker side and mine of a happy-go-lucky wanderer. It had been a strange encounter at first. Her words chosen more to shock than explain, and mine more of fantasy than reality, but after a while she felt at ease and the light-hearted hustler in her surfaced. She was an expert at playing the teasing game. Her moves were calculated and the more I tried to look away the more she reeled me in. She was more than tough. Her freelance work had made her wary, smart beyond her years, and her sixth sense at what buttons to press gave her an insight into male behaviour that many a housewife would envy. She told of the big time,'indoors' as she put it. Pre-booked hotel rooms, photo shoots, stretched limousines and endless parties. Then the cold hard reality of last night's truckies brought her back to street level. She was like my alter ego. All the things I wish I had done, but hadn't. All those solo experiences and all those hours spent on the road instead of bars. She must have read my thoughts.

"Like it?" She had released the hook of her coat. I was sinking, I hung onto her eyes like a drowning man.

"I like you, you're nice." She was laughing. I was landed and she knew it. Her hand hooked mine. I was transported. I remember the cold air, her impish smile and the touch of her skin. She held me and I cried. All those months of mental and physical pain. She uncorked me like a bottle of vintage champagne, stayed with me just the time it took for its bubbles to burst, then left me weak and limp by the rickshaw.

Names, like songs, can provoke all kinds of memories that remind us exactly where we were and what was going on in our lives at the time we heard them. Who were you dating when Dave Henderson scored the winning goal in the '72 Canada Cup and where is Woodstock? They are all events that stick in your mind. They were all given world wide attention at the time, but there is one name, I left out. He epitomizes guts and determination, and back in 1980, an article hidden away in the back pages of the Toronto Star would leave me with a lasting impression. He's long since passed into folklore. They've erected statues and named schools and highways after him. His name is Terry Fox. He died of cancer. His Trans Canada Run on one leg was cut short just east of Thunder Bay and his friendly ghost still haunts me.

Since Victoria, I had thought of how often people had tried to cross Canada and who, through illness, time constraint, or just plain fatigue, had given up. Terry had put crossing Canada on the map, but sadly, too many copycats were spoiling it. The summer airways had been full of registered charities and causes making the crossing shielded by their army of minders. I had met a person walking for Aids just outside Vancouver, another from the Rainbow Alliance in Calgary and the Heart Foundation was sponsoring a Cross Canada Relay Run which I expected to see any day on the road. Outside one German cyclist, two Japanese and one American, I hadn't met one Canadian making the crossing just for the hell of it, and I was begining to think I was the only one.

The first time you arrive at a destination with no money it's scary. The second time it's old hat. The third time you crave its rush and from then on you're hooked. I'd arrived in Thunder Bay with the promise of money and left it until the last day to check it out. I should have known better, but the older I get, the lazier I get. I had already spent four days on a spending binge, and that morning I left the Youth Hostel for the Post Office with only one hundred and fifty dollars to my name and over three thousand kilometers to go.

"No, Mr Howgate, we have no mail for you."

Oh God! I was getting too old for this excitement. I know we live in an age of 24 hour instant tellers, plastic cards and bank pass books, but I have never joined the ride. I still use general delivery, registered letters and travellers cheques and when all else fails, the phone booth.

Behind any successful venture, there's a team of backseat supporters. Mine were my friends. The back-slapping optimistic type of armchair travellers that I could call on to do my dirty work. They paid my forgotten bills, returned my calls and babysat my ego. When I left Toronto in April. I had cut the umbilical cord. I had closed my bank account, given up my apartment and left a shopping list of contact dates and places with friends. In Toronto, I was as regular and as predictable as the next man, but on the road, I am a different animal.

"Hi Tom, it's Bernie."

Tom was my Old Reliable. We had known each other for over sixteen years. He was my banker so to speak. Money transactions to him were old hat. In the past,he'd wired me money to Australia, India and Africa. All I had to do was pick up the phone, reverse the charges and give him the details. I didn't have to plead, make up a lame excuse or fabricate a lie. Tom knew the moment my voice registered down the phone lines what I wanted.

"Don't tell me, Bernie. You want some money." What are friends for if you can't use them occasionally?

I left Thunder Bay head down with only speed on my mind. I was cruising, in a groove and the miles were just flying by when..!
Wow...wow...wow...wow...wow...wow...wow... wow...
Suddenly the silence shattered. Out of nowhere came the cat's meow. It did a U'y, accelerated, then screeched to a halt in front of me. 'What the hell?' I didn't say it, but I thought it. I braked, skidded, then sunk into the soft shoulder. At first the blue and white didn't register. Then the driver's uniform spoke for him. Not long out of puberty, his face had that soft pink

puffy look that rarely sees blades. They had sent a boy to do a man's job. Innocent to the point of being nervous, his eyes fell everywhere except mine. I'd been told the RCMP blooded their new recruits in the north, but no one had told me just how young.

"Do you have a license for this vehicle, sir?" Was he serious? Half eaten to death by black fly and suffering from a mild case of sun stroke, I was in no mood for small talk.

"Did you shave this morning or do you always look so good?" He didn't even rise to the bait.

"We've had complaints about slow moving vehicles, sir."

"What an astute observation, son." At last he bit. The word 'son' touched a nerve. I was immediately broadsided. First he hit me with rules and regulations, then floored me with roadside etiquette. He was warming to his job and the more he talked, the taller he stood. I was biding my time, playing out the rope, waiting for the right moment to yank him back.

"It's a bicycle, officer." The word bicycle stopped him in his tracks. "No, correction, it's a rickshaw. You might call it a pedi-cab. It's got one gear, weighs over two hundred pounds and is powered by these...." I was pointing to my legs. "Can I continue?" His face fell. At last the dime had dropped. He took time out. I could see the cogs moving slowly behind his eyes.

"Sorry sir, but we have to check everything. Sightseers in slow moving vehicles cause most of the accidents on this section." His face relaxed into a smile. The boy in him had returned and there was a spring in his step, then just before he got into his car,

"Would you like to join me, sir?"

"Why?" I asked.

"Because it's air-conditioned," he said with a laugh. The ice broken, we both laughed. He called base. Gave them his position, then offered me some of his mother's homemade blueberry pie.

I made Nipigon before nightfall, spent the evening debating which route to take east. Highway 11 to Cochrane or Highway 17 to Sault Ste. Marie, then left the decision to sleep.

Chapter 11
Lake Superior

For those who have never seen Lake Superior, you get an inadequate picture of it when you hear it called a lake. And for those who have sailed over it, the term lake must sound ludicrous. It may be fresh and crystal clear, but it breeds storms with the same force as any salt water ocean.

My first view of its waters were in Thunder Bay and, since Nipigon, I had been keeping my eyes out for its elusive horizon. I had chosen Highway 17 to the Sault over the smoother, less travelled route to Cochrane because of its promised scenery, but I was paying an early price.

At Rossport the road cut inland for 5 kilometres. I cycled to the crest of a high plateau, then without notice its bottom fell out. Below the valley broadened. The road dropped, blurred behind spruce trees, then lost itself to a sea of green. For the best part of the day, I'd been on and off the rickshaw, pushing, pulling and peddling with nothing but trees, rock and the occasional spoiled view of Lake Superior, but the distant hill promised a better horizon.

As I climbed, I could hear sea gulls. For thirty minutes time crawled, then a sudden blast of air and I was on top. I turned into the breeze and instinctively looked down. What a sight. There at my feet, stretching out to a haze on the horizon was Superior. It was beautiful. An opal sheet of water unspoiled by islands and as large as an ocean. I had been travelling so slowly that these sudden views were a rarity. I had followed the contours of Lake Superior from Nipigon but its outline was always blurred by objects. Nine times out of ten the speedy traveller misses these subtleties, but there are times when speed is better and the faster the picture it flashes the more memorable they become. This sudden flash was like a towel dropped. That sudden nudity. The unannounced view that stamps itself in your mind in a way prolonged association rarely achieves. It seduced me off my bike, took me over a well worn trail and led me onto a secluded beach.

A small brook flowed quietly into the lake. I heard a fish jump. The waters were crisp and cold, but tempting. I thought about it for a moment, then before I knew it, I was stripped and air born.

Holy Christ! My head exploded, blood thickened, toes curled and there was a wrinkle where my sex used to be. I butterflied back in one stroke and cleared the bank in one movement. I had never moved so fast in my life. There's nothing like a cool dip to sobber one up. I was dressed and back in the saddle in no time. And that night, seduced by an offering of a warm meal in Terrace Bay, I showered the remaining cool spots of my experience in needles of piping hot water.

At Marathon, I paid the price for my tentless nomadic lifestyle. I was forced to cut short my day in a thunderstorm, take refuge in a disused trailer only to be woken after midnight by its local drunk. In White River, under a star-filled sky, I had another night of human interruption, this time from the carnal sounds of a courting couple in its baseball diamond. I was beginning to miss the natural music of outdoor living. I was too close to civilization. This stretch of the Trans Canada didn't even offer a postage stamp of clear dry ground to camp on and where were the deserted beaches when I needed them?

In the wilderness constants don't frighten me. A bear, a moose or even a timid timber wolf may lurk just out of sight within spitting distance of a busy road and you wouldn't even know.

At the foot of a great forest or on the shores of a vast lake, man is the arch-enemy from whom nature flees. Animals distinguish instantly the slightest noise made by man and even a chocolate bar wrapping could be looked upon as a booby trap.The laughing owls may hoot, a crow screech, a beaver awaken the dead with a resounding smack of its tail on water, or a moose walk carelessly along, rattling the underbrush, but let man so much as break a twig and all living creatures within earshot will, each according to his kind, sink beneath the surface of water, fade sound-lessly into the shadows, leap and bound for cover or freeze like a cat. I had learned from past mistakes to be still, quiet and, above all,unafraid. Patience, as any hunter will tell you, has its rewards. Animals, after all, are as curious as humans. A moose may be big and timid, but it has an incurable curiosity to match its humungous snout. A bear will feel he owns the land you're on and pride will force him out into the open if only to prove a point. Large animals look to the sky for warnings and their smaller neighbours for gossip. If you can get their trust, the battle is half won. The crow is a pushover, a natural show-off. It craves an audi-ence and to be ignored is its worst form of punish-ment. Squirrels just want to know how fast you climb trees. Beavers are work-a-holics and can't go long without a fix. Only the wolves, the true hunters of the wilderness, the wolverine, its prime scavenger; and the cat family are elusive, and who in their right mind wants to face them down buck naked in a sleeping bag? Patience is the name of the game and after a while you just become another piece of furniture, but like anything in life, there are exceptions to the rule and two immediately come to mind. The porcupine and the skunk. It would seem that when the brains were handed out, these two were absent from class. To them, strange noises or the smell of cooking are like music and ambrosia and no sooner would I make camp when one or the other would appear.

The porcupine, fat and rotund with a coat of oversized needles to carry, has an appetite befitting its girth and will attack anything that's not nailed down, hung from a great height or under lock and key. I've even heard of them gnawing holes in canoes and delighting in dried paint. Leather goods are a specialty. In fact, anything made of canvas, wood or paper, all the essentials a happy camper needs for shelter, warmth and security. And he's not past leaving a few barb quills at the dinner table just for fun. But for all his bad habits, he's harmless.

The skunk is also friendly, too friendly in fact. They have this inbuilt community spirit that drives them to be around humans in a way that only a house cat would understand, and with that same need for closeness that puts a cat on your lap, I've woken to find them curled up against my mosquito net on the back seat of my rickshaw and rummaging through my

clothes bag. Three times I have come close to being perfumed by their scent and in my book that's three times too many.

For the uninitiated, Canada's wildlife can be frightening and ferocious in pursuit of prey, but all have their moments. I've witnessed bears rolling in the snow and a bobcat stretched out to the limit doing early morning calisthenics. Have you ever heard a beaver in conversation? If they could swim half as fast as they chatter, they would own every water speed record known to man. Who couldn't help laughing at otters at play; ducks on the mate, or the sound of woodpeckers wakening the dead. Is there a better sight than a half-crazed, sex-starved moose on the rut? I've seen baby deer with legs ten times bigger than their brains trying to stand, and all you have to do is look skyward on a breezy day and watch hawks flying in the wind only for the express purpose of riding its currents on speedy races going nowhere. How can a person ever forget the haunting sound of a loon crying to its mate at sunset, the spine-chilling sound of a wild cat's scream, or the lone howl of a wolf during full moon? And you have never lived until you've dined at the table of blue jays whose table manners would even put a hungry hoard of children fighting over the last cookie to shame. Is Bernie ever bored? Not likely.

I was now cycling through that typically North American experience; towns born into the boom-and-bust syndrome, with school reunions often better remembered than lived in. My route had already taken me to half-a-dozen lakeside communities and there were many more to come. Most had boasted larger populations than they now housed. Mines and pulp mills had sprouted up like mushrooms in the boom years proceeding the Great War, but many more had shaved their productions and some even mothballed them. It wasn't as if they were ghost towns, far from it. Miners had been replaced by artisans, forest workers by retirees, but the threads that held them together, its schools, churches and bars, had long since emptied. Boarded-up homes, abandoned trailer courts and stores for sale told their own story. For some, communities like Kenora, Dryden, Nipigon and Terrace Bay had taken root, expanded, diversified and been able to buffer the winds of change. The bustling days when Superior surfed the crest of an 'Energy, Mines and Resources' wave had disappeared into folk lore. I knew Marathon and Elliot Lake had seen better days, and Timmins and Sudbury to the east were also suffering. I knew mines existed just north and south of the highway, but many of the small towns they fed seemed derelict and sad; if not yet ghost towns, then allowed to exist through the social insurance stamp and retirement benefits. They now relied, like so many I had seen in British Columbia, on tourism. Nurturing its past through industrial museums and selling futures through packaging heritage sights into manicured tracks of wilderness.

Some of these towns have built thriving tourist industries around myths. For instance, in Ignace I was told everybody heads to the town's garbage dump at sunset to watch the bears, and in White River, no trip along the Trans Canada Highway is complete without a pilgrimage to its local A&W, where one can be pictured standing next to a huge thermometer to commemorate its place as Ontario's coldest spot. And now in Wawa it was a huge sculptured Canada Goose.

From Wawa, the road cut a course through the scenic lakeside buffs of Superior National Park. I had spent three glorious days of laid-back hospitality in Wawa and was now looking for a fix of excitement. I had stopped at the top of a rise. The view of Superior was breathtaking, but its glazed sheen of water wasn't what interested me. Ahead and below, the road dipped, switched back behind a sheer slab of rock, then dropped hundreds of feet into a carpet of green. It was that sharp edge of fear that I was looking for. The view had already untapped my adrenalin and its taste came up the back of my throat. I now readied myself for a rush of blood. Like sky-diving, there is a moment of no return and twenty seconds into my descent I'd passed it.

Suddenly the sky arced. The sun disappeared into a green haze, then silence. The next I remember was a warm sensation tickling the back of my neck, then the drums started. The cut wasn't deep, but the blood flowed like a river. I was more embarrassed than hurt and more worried that my bike had broken in half than my head might have split in two.

By noon, I'd had enough. The question posed by the grating noise in my pedal crank far outweighed the noises in my head. At Superior National Park H.Q., I stopped to speak to a warden. I had expected a thick set, muscle-bound type, but instead was pleasantly surprised. The last time I had visited a National Park was in the late '70s during an infamous 'long weekend' of revelry. That time two park wardens, not long out of puberty but built like pocket battleships, had been called to break up a dawn 'til dusk party. They had been outnumbered twelve to one, but their size more than made up the difference. Stretched-at-birth, those two lads, until today, had been my only yard stick to gauge a park warden. I was just wondering what tactic this young freckled-face nymph would have used, when she broke my train of thought.

"I think you will find all the tools you require to fix your bike in our Park's garage. If you have any problems ask for Chris or Stef."

If ever I have had my chauvinistic ears pinned back against a wall, and had my inflated ego punctured, the dynamic duo of Chris and Stef did it. They assaulted my eyes from the word go and in sixty minutes these two under-dressed, sweat and greased up to their elbows and shorts up to their student crotches had my rickshaw stripped, oiled cleaned and put back together before what they had done even registered. They shattered the 'bambi doll' stereotype, I had carried since childhood and then some. When you don't have children, travel as much as I do and skirt the winds of change, you tend to live in a time warp. It's not that I couldn't keep eye contact, it was the familiarity with which they handled the tools of their trade. It wasn't the crash bang wallop, sports illustrated swim suit calendar decorated scene of my youth, but one of finesse, warmth and touch of philosophy. In sixty minutes, I passed through two generations, a condensed course in feminism that didn't once threaten castration or impinge on my male privileges. I didn't so much enjoy their presence as feel that I had been seduced through a crack in the wall, and when I turned to leave and Chris jokingly shouted, 'nice pair of buns', they made my day.

By late afternoon the sky had turned clear blue. The air had stilled and Superior's surface was like glass. I'd not meant to stop. I was at the top of a rise just outside Montreal River surrounded by heavy bush, and every shadow looked to have its quota of mosquitoes. I had put in six cycling days since leaving Thunder Bay on the shore line of Lake Superior, but not once camped down by its beaches. Saulte Ste. Marie was just around the corner. From there on in, I knew it would be nose-to-tail traffic in comparison to what I was leaving. I wanted one last lakeside experience and there was no time like the present.

I changed roadside, slipped into my nylon training trousers, put on my long sleeve sweater, then pushed the bike off the road and behind some trees for security. The next thirty minutes was spent searching for a good camping spot. I chose a rock bluff carpeted in ferns, then set about building a fire.

What a fire I made. It cracked and sparkled and illuminated half the beach in the dimming light. The sky had turned from royal blue to bronze and as its colours disappeared, Superior's waters turned from silver to oily black. The night sky was only freckled. It still hadn't turned its lights on when two loons sang to me. A lone hawk rode an updraft and a squadron of geese landed in a flurry of chatter. I lay back, not caring about the whine of mosquitoes. I was in a different world. I was dreaming, stroking the night sky with my thoughts and breathing in the damp sweet smells of the early evening air. "Could there be any better place?", I thought, then..........!!

Wop...wop...wop...wop...wop...wop...wop...wop...wop. One by one, cottage generators kicked-in, until the night's silence turned into that of an inner city and the peninsula's beautiful dark silhouettes suddenly turned into a Christmas tree of light.

Chapter 12
Welcome to the real world

Shared travel experiences for me hold as much currency as sex does to a hooker. Repetition can be boring. Most of it is back-slapping one-upmanship, but my nights spent in Sault Ste. Marie's cosy little youth hostel, shared among kindred spirits, was like a breath of fresh air. I needed the rest. From here on it would be all down hill. Welcome to the real world.

The route to Sudbury was a strange mixture of flat, straight causeway borded by forest and steep inclines mushroomed with rock. The sweet smells of nature were now being choked by a steady flow of car fumes, and settlements were only hours apart. Rush hour was a constant headache. 7:00 a.m. to 8:00 a.m., noon till 1:00 p.m. and 5:00 p.m. to 7:00 p.m. At the Elliot Lake turn-off, I was almost decapitated by a loose pipe hanging off the side of a truck. And just out-side Espanola a speeding car side-swiped me into a ditch. I had already bitten my nails down to the bone, had a strong case of lock-jaw in my knuckles and was now grinding my teeth down to the gum. At Whitefish, I stopped for one beer, stretched it into five and fell asleep within spitting distance of the pub's front door. I was a nervous wreck. In fact the only bright light I could speak of since leaving the Sault was the increased booty of goodies I found roadside. Since leaving Victoria, I had picked up half a dozen wrench-es, a Black and Decker power tool, two screw drivers,

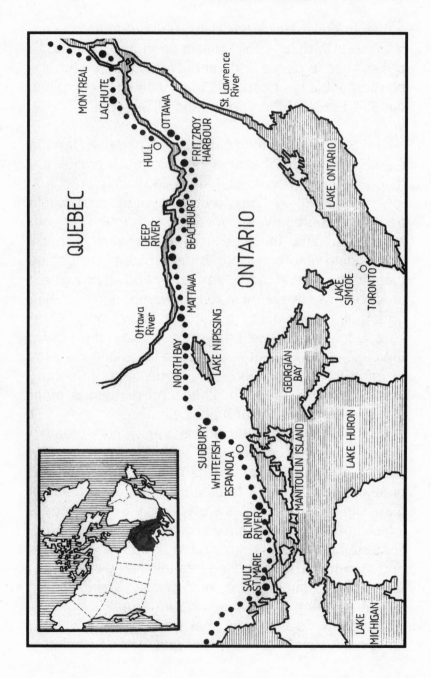

a twenty dollar bill, a transistor radio, numerous sunglasses, a watch, a coin collection in excess of $5, a dozen license plates and I could have made a fortune on refundable beer cans. All in all, I couldn't complain, but still, I missed the open roads of Superior.

Sudbury, the rock capital of Canada. In Canada there is too much of everything. Too much prairie, too much mountain, too much tundra, too much forest and too much water. I know some countries that would bankrupt themselves for only a fraction of our resources. What most people fail to realize is that it isn't finding resources that is the problem, it's getting them to the market place. You rarely find anything next to roads. It's always over some swamp, under a lake, on top of a mountain or just too far away from civilization. Occasionally, we strike accessible riches or, in the case of Sudbury, it was just too large and too easy to mine to pass up and, to a large degree, Sudbury made Timmins and Elliot Lake and numerous other mines in Northern Ontario possible.

Sudbury was and still is the world's greatest nickel mine and, depending on your point of view, Ontario's sweaty armpit or its heart. Recent outside pressure has forced it to clean up its act, but still its mine site more resembles a breakers yard than a geological masterpiece. Smoke stacks rise like huge erections, but unstable markets have doused their flames and their half empty parking lots tell their own story.

"Best damn place in Canada." These words greeted me in a donut shop on Elm Street.

"How do you work that one out, mate?" He'd hung out his statement like bait and, when I nibbled it, was all the excuse he needed to toss out more.

"We know where we stand, which is more than most." I spent sixty minutes in the donut shop. Five minutes talking and fifty-five minutes listening. I was treated in that time to a layman's lesson on Canada's heritage, its resources, their wealth and fall-out, but most of all Sudbury's place on the map and its eminent importance to the world of minerals.

"Who cares if a few hundred miles of wilderness gets polluted. We're just a blip on the horizon. Look around you. Our back yard stretches clear to the Arctic." His arguments may not have been dotted with large words, and his facts and figures may not have come from the pages of the Financial Post, but this man knew his stuff.

"We know better than outsiders what we live in. Pollution, give me pollution any day over the dole. Some sensitive bugger in a cottage down wind of the stack started all this pollution stuff." He'd dug his heels in and he wouldn't move. There was more than a tinge of humour in his voice. No doubt longterm residents of Hell eventually adjust, I thought. It was always the old-timers, the ones that remembered the good times. The families that stuck it out through thick and thin. Those unseen committee members that ran the local baseball and hockey teams and their women that kept the community blood pumping round. He told me that recent cutbacks and volunteer retirees had weeded out the last of the 'social climbers' and 'cowboys' as he put them. "We're down to the bone now. The ones that are left are the ones that want to stay here. We're not just a mine site, we're a community." I found in his words the two qualities of honesty and economy that had typified my travels through isolated communities. From Golden in B.C. to Flin Flon in Manitoba, around Superior and now northern Ontario's mining districts. They all had forged the same characters and my first hour in Sudbury set the seal for a pleasant stay.

I had arrived at the height of Sudbury's 'Blue Berry Festival' and the streets were crowded and in festive spirits. A phone call on arrival, passed on from the Sault, and new friends arrived on queue. Once again the underground travellers network of friends had turned up trumps.

From Sudbury, I took the short hop to North Bay and to a junction of major decision. When I first planned this trip, Toronto had been a major pit stop. The plan had been to rest up there, visit friends and take time out before continuing east to Newfoundland, but things had changed much in the last few months. I was slowly becoming public property. The 15-second news bites of British Columbia were now stretching into full blown news items and the press had moved my rickshaw from the back page to the front. I now had a list of radio, television and newspaper contacts as long as your arm and I was beginning to feel an unwanted pressure to succeed.

I was now getting flagged down on a regular basis. My rickshaw had been framed, videoed and sound-recorded at every stop. I was posing with wives, husbands and children at every turn and a feeling not unlike the visiting politician with the plastic smile was pinching a nerve. One couple, having heared of my trip via a CBC. 'Radio North' interview in Flin Flon, made a 400-mile round trip from Churchill just to see the 'Bike Man' and another who had tuned into Vicky Gabereau had even built a long weekend around meeting me. My trip 'Newfie or Bust', as one CBC. interviewer coined it, had caught the public's imagination and the John and Jane Smiths of this world now wanted a flicker of its flame. Local cycle groups chased me down. I couldn't even go for a piss without being spotted and everyone from the Rotary Club to the Women's League wanted a piece of the story. I had been given an address book of contacts to see, stay or just plain party with. The element of spontaneity I loved so much at the beginning was disappearing fast. I was becoming a media event looking for escape and finding less and less space in which to manoeuvre. Toronto was out of the question. I may think I am one, but I am no media star. I can't hack the pressure of time constraints. Big cities expect their pound of flesh and if you are late for an appointment it's a case of today's news is tomorrow's history. I like small town flexibility, their cosy environment and laid back ways. I had already stayed in the homes of three newspaper reporters, been invited to a television crew's end of day party in Calgary, but in Toronto I would be treated as just another crazy doing his thing and would be interviewed accordingly.

My decision was actually made weeks earlier, but not until I reached the junction of Highways 17 and 11 in North Bay, did it become a reality. I made Mattawa on the banks of the Ottawa River by sunset and by the following night, I was camping under the disc of a full moon, serenaded by the noise of tennis balls within striking distance of the club house in Deep River, en route to Ottawa.

The scenery once again changed at Pembroke. The corridor of forest that closed its pages on leaving Winnipeg over three weeks before, now opened like the pages of a book. Trees melted into pasture, corn fields and cash crops. Narrowly fertile, as all river basins are, the land surrounding the Ottawa River was too flat to be picturesque, but sufficiently rolling to seduce me off the Trans Canada and onto its secondary roads through Beachburg. Stately elms fanned out in all directions, and here and there history surfaced. Stone cottages, farms of red brick and Dutch barns. Once again the small corner stores offered more than limp spotted fruit and the roadside gardens, manicured with exotic flowers, bore evidence to a culture more rooted in permanence and pleasure than one of survival and utility. The hard crust of Superior had sanded down to the smooth surface of civilized life styles. Muscle cars with tires as big as doorways and topped with a barrage of spotlights had given way to the compact Lincolns and Mercedes of old money. Tourists now shot with cameras, not guns and the dirt and stained jean look of manual labour had been replaced by the design tear look of boutiques.

It was Sunday, and it was as if Ottawa had pulled the plugs out, and every dysfunctional family with wheels were draining down the roads. I was now having to compete for those out-of-the-way pit stops with hormonally-imbalanced pre-teens attached to warp '10' stereo systems and tiny tots with vocal chords to match. The pressure cooker of city life was escaping everywhere and I was getting an earful.

I chose the sleepy little village of Fritzroy Harbour for my last stop before Ottawa. I camped in its

United Church grounds, fell asleep within earshot of its practicing choir, but the thought of waking up to the Monday morning rush hour wasn't a pleasant one.

What can I say about Ottawa except beautifully boring? Ottawa is typical of all capital cities; too many chiefs and not enough Indians. A world within a world, it's the only place in Canada where political news can be found in the entertainment section. Ottawa had been a "must" stop from the word go. My benefactor, the Pakistani Ambassador to Canada, had given me specific instructions to call in en route to Newfoundland, and ambassadorial requests cannot be snubbed easily.

To fully appreciate my state of mind on the morning I arrived at the embassy gates, you have to understand that for over four months I had been the centre of attraction-or at the very least my rickshaw had-and after a while you tend to believe your own press cuttings.

'THE BIKE MAN COMETH'
'HOWGATE'S CYCLING ODYSSEY'
'ADVENTURER HITS THE ROAD AGAIN'
'WORLD IN HIS POCKET'

They went on and on. From Victoria B.C. to Ottawa, I had been the breath of fresh air that interviewers loved to interview. I was beginning to feel like Gulliver in the land of Lilliput. Ten foot tall with shoulders to match. I wasn't quite at the walk-on-water stage, but I was getting there. I had arrived at the embassy totally unannounced. I wanted to surprise them. I had even purchased a new pair of running shoes and was wearing freshly laundered shorts and sweater for the occasion. I had entered the embassy on the crest of a wave. I was shooting straight for the top. No middle men for Bernie. I strutted up to the security counter with an air of confidence fit for a king and rattled out my request to see the Ambassador as if we were bosom buddies. I wanted to see the Ambassador now, and I wouldn't take no for an answer.

I should have read the writing on the wall when two 'Rocky" look-alikes turned up with matching Calvin Klein shades. They didn't so much ask me to follow them as use the quiet persuasion of their size. How was I to know the whole place was on security alert? Could I be blamed if I looked like some Muslim Fundamentalist?

I began to panic when they left me in a small bare room to look at my mirrored reflection. For what felt like an eternity, I was left to sweat it out. Had I turned left instead of right? Was this the 'People's Republic of Libya's Embassy'? Was I to be drugged, embalmed, crated and ransomed? God. I had the makings of a best seller on my hands. Who wants to read about a boring old cycling trip when the Arabian Nights beckoned. I was into my final chapter. I could picture my release live on CNN and negotiating pub-lishing rights with Faber & Faber, when a cup of spiced tea broke my dream.

"Sorry, Mr. Howgate. We can't be too careful. We have been receiving a lot of telephone threats against the Ambassador's person in the last few weeks. I have spoken to his secretary about your request. Unfortunately, the Ambassador is out of town this week, but we have arranged an interview for you with the CBC."

What, no golden handshake? No state dinner. No tuxedo. In your dreams, Bernie. I left with my tail between my legs, scooted over to CBC, taped my thirty-second news bite, then cycled over the Ottawa River and into Quebec.

Chapter 13
La Belle Province

It's hard to fathom another society, especially when it's supposed to be part of yours. For starters, its language has a rhythm all of its own. I've heard it called the language of love. It has verbs that conjugate. Nouns that can be both male and female and a delivery that bares the soul.

"Vous parlez anglais, si vous plait?"

Not bad for starters, but unfortunately my French stretched no further. My first conversation was more animated than vocal. I'd stopped at the first *depanneur* on leaving Hull for smokes, received my first '*lecon de francais*' and ended up staying for lunch. Well, so much for my initial script. I had been warned that without a basic understanding of French, I would be lost, at the very least cold-shouldered. I had expected a chilly reception, only to find that actions speak louder than words.

For the next one-and-a-half days, I was lulled into a false sense of security. Scrums punctuated my every stop. The sight of my rickshaw emptied a roadside school, gave entrance to a garden barbecue on the shores of the Ottawa River and by day's end, passport to an evening between clean sheets. Quebec's true colours, or should I say road etiquette, didn't hit me until the bottom half of day two.

No one, and I do mean no one, jay walks for

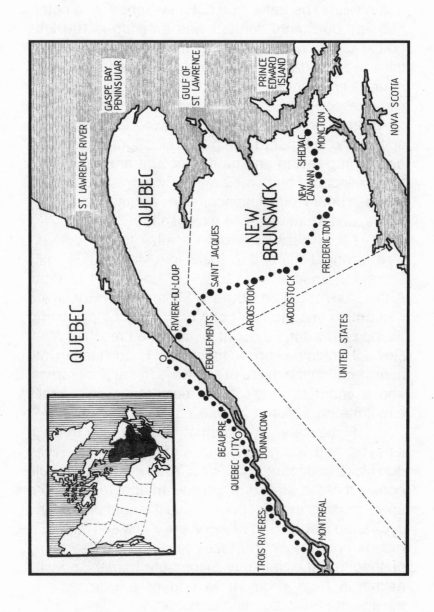

pleasure in Montreal unless you're drunk or have a death wish. The traffic had not only turned up a notch, but was downright scary. I was entering a 100 k/hr. gridlock with nobody getting anywhere. Those who think war is dangerous have not experienced rush hour traffic, Quebec style. Montreal is a city of two million stressed-out people who daily use its road system as a huge pressure valve. All driving is done at top speed and bumper to bumper. Traffic lights are excuses for drag racing and on no account are traffic cops to be minded. I had timed my entry to miss rush hour, but rush hour North American-style means twenty-four hours, and Montreal is no exception.

I look back now and it's easy to see where I went wrong. I planned to sneak into Montreal using its secondary roads. I was to follow Route 334 to Point Arthur, turn south on Route 148 then follow Boulevard Laurentien into the heart of Montreal, but that's as far as the plan went. I thought by the time I reached Mont Royal, I would be spoiled for choice. I hadn't taken into consideration the maze of slip-ways, on and off ramps, and a concrete jungle of barriers that would finally direct me onto Montreal's busiest six lane highway.

Picture a snail underfoot, then see life through its eyes, and you get a glimpse of my paranoia. They don't take prisoners in Quebec. You can throw the rule book out of the window when you enter a freeway. The only firm rules are that trucks have the right of way and cycles are illegal. Speed signs are jokes and 'ARRET' means only the time it takes to read it. I was being pushed into the traffic by a concrete barrier and with neither a hard shoulder to hug or a side walk to escape on, I was courting disaster.

One kilometer into my nightmare, my nerves were shredded. Abuse was coming thick and fast.

CLUNK..THUD..SCREECH..

A down changing gear, a blast of noise and suddenly I was caught in a whirlpool of wind and shadow. I scraped the concrete barrier. A mirror snapped. The air was full of diesel and the noise deafening. I saw eight huge wheels pass, then my maker, then the sky. I'd had enough. I got off the rickshaw. Retraced my route all the way back to the slip-way. Exited the freeway and did what I should have done long ago; bought a street map. I found my friend's apartment in Lachine in no time, then fast forwarded the day's events with a bottle of wine.

Montreal deserted on a damp Sunday has a life all of its own. The sound of church bells and hang-outs at street cafes are what life is all about. I remember my first visit to Montreal in '76. It was the year of the Olympics. The Parti Quebecois was in power and the chain smoking Rene Levesque was at its helm. The atmosphere was as bubbly as champagne. Girls were not only beautiful, but sexy with a capital S. Conversations were filled with politics and emotions ran high. Walls were collapsing. It was a time of change. Youth was flexing its muscles and virgin ideas taking root. Bars were electric and the air was thick with the soft perfumes of attraction. It was easy to rub up against a new experience. Like sex first time around, in Montreal that year, its shape, fashion and smell left an indelible imprint. Today, I found it a sad memory. That distinct society of my youth was no more. Montreal in the '90s had entered into a contest with Toronto and was beating it at its own game. Rene Levesque's distinct society had been sold to the highest bidder. They had entered the big leagues and the freshness and fire of his era had turned into a brash, arrogant, money-orientated society. I now found St. Denis, once the centre of Montreal's artistic subculture, had turned into a postcard memory of gift shops.

What had once been a scruffy but authentic historical neighbourhood had turned into a sanitized tourist attraction. Houses that fifteen years ago hung signs 'chambre a louer' in their windows now called themselves hotels. Street side cafes that once overlapped, had lost their freedom to side-walk cages. Expensive face-lifts had brushed away much of the area's uniqueness, which now looked no different in character than Toronto's high class Yorkville. The worst instincts of Quebec nationalism had purged everything into a boring 'yuppified' sameness.

'Je me souviens'. I remember what? Even its license plates had been usurped. Quebec used to be 'La Belle Province'. Today the fiery independent generation who had fought dearly to retain its culture had been pushed aside, but not all the changes were bad. The Lachine Canal had been given a face-lift and the cycle path which follows its course from Lachine to Montreal Harbour was a Godsend. Without cars to contend with, the cycle path looked bigger than it actually was. A jogger passed, then a group of skin tight spandex on wheels. I rounded a courting couple, an old lady with a dog, then was detoured by a vendor selling coffee. I saw roller bladers, pedestrians with walkmans, kite flyers, baby strollers and ripened flesh tanned by the sun. The scenes were warm and pleasant. You could almost reach out and touch the skyscrapers, and the freeways were only dull throbbing reminders that you were within the city limits. The canal ran slow and peaceful and the dry grass, shaded by the trees was inviting. It was late afternoon. I had been out since 7:00 a.m. taking in the sights and I was tired.

Just before Lachine, the cycle path narrowed, rose through a corridor of trees,crested, then dropped. That's when it happened! My brakes failed. In front was a woman with a pram. I now had three choices: the canal, the railway tracks or a tree. I didn't want to get wet and I'm no train enthusiast, so I chose the tree.

I wasn't going fast when I hit it; 5 Ks tops, but it was enough. The rickshaw went one way, I went another. Back on my feet, I checked for damage. My handlebar, always a bit wobbly, nearly came off in my hands and now my front wheel was tight up against its fender. Try as I may, I couldn't bend it back. Whoever put the rickshaw together knew his stuff. I took the offending fender off, went back along the pathway and found the problem brake pad and ended having to half push, and half carry, lifting the front wheel all the way back to my friend's apartment in Lachine.

The accident had pushed my alarm bells. Repairing punctures and making simple adjustments were one thing, but having to wrap my mind around anything more complicated was quite a different proposition. I spent most of that evening counting nuts, chasing ball bearings across the floor and beating the hell out of my handle bar stem. The front handle bar support rods had taken the accident's force, transferred it down the stem and the rest was history. I now needed divine intervention or a good repair man.

For six hours my rickshaw held out against all the high-tech knowledge of two bike shops, but third time turned out lucky. I hit upon a bright spark: a young man with more cycle savvy than selling power to come up with the solution.

"Cooking foil. I took the stem out, wrapped some foil around it, then stuffed it back in. I've straightened the stem up the best I could, even filed it down a bit, because you told me you pull it up the hills and put a lot of strain on the handle bars. I thought it would be better to be too tight than too loose."

He was just what the doctor ordered. Not only

did he fix, grease and oil all my parts, but before leaving, he disassembled the handle bar stem and repacked it with foil just to show me how it was done. I now had just one more stop to make before leaving Montreal.

St. Catherine Street has the reputation of being one of the gayest and wickedest stretches of real estate in Canada. It's a place where God and the Devil meet on equal footing. Where religious houses of worship compete on a daily basis for custom on one side of the street with XXX movie theatres on the other. Traffic down St. Catherine's was a 20 K/hr. nightmare of automobile window shopping with nobody getting anywhere fast and its side walks were endless matches of pushing and shoving. I was heading for the corner of St. Catherine's and Atwater I was on a pilgrimage which no self-respecting hockey enthusiast could pass up before leaving Montreal. I was on my way to visit the Forum. While some countries have gone to war over such trivial matters of land, food and shelter, Quebecers take to the trenches every Saturday to watch their heroes, Les Canadiens, carry their flag of pride onto the ice to do battle. The Forum had an atmosphere all its own. Pictures of past heroes look down at you from every wall and banners hang from the roof like a much-decorated soldier. To understand Quebec's psyche you have to understand the Forum's shrine-like importance. Hockey is just not a sport in Quebec, but a collective expression of pride. North America is inhabited by over 260 million English-speaking people and Quebec with its six million Francophones doesn't even qualify for the status as junior partner, but its hockey club gives it a continen-

tal platform par excellence. Once a year millions of
North Americans tune into the Stanley Cup Finals and
more often than not Les Canadiens are front and centre. Ask anyone south of the border, "Who is the
Canadian Prime Minister?" and you will be met by a
blank expression. But ask anyone from the cities of
Boston, New York, Detriot or Chicago who is Guy
Lafleur, Rocket Richard or Guy Charboneau, and you
will get an answer five times out of ten.

By early evening, I was cradling a glass of
wine. The sun had set on my last night in Montreal and
I had returned to St. Denis to rekindle my old love
affair with it. It was a hazy summer night. Above the
sky was pitch black. The restaurants of St. Denis had
emptied of their daily specials and were now readying
themselves for a different menu. Eye contact now
replaced business conversation and, mating calls,
were replacing formal greetings. The streets were filling with the fashion conscious, and their quota of
biceps. Some constants never change. Couples held
hands, linked arms and exchanged pocket holds.
Some weaved, some bobbed, and groups hunting in
packs lingered. I was just about to head home when I
spotted two girls staring at me. They were wearing
those loosely fitting short skirts that sail in the wind.
Their legs were golden, slender and long. I was
hooked and landed before I knew it, and was soon
paying for the privilege.

At last Montreal smiled on me and, with two
beautiful girls as guides, I wound my way through its
back streets. Me cycling, they sat cuddled up in youthful enthusiasm on the passenger's seat, waving at
friends, screaming out commands. *Arret, a droit, a*

gauche, but most of all, sharing their love of the city and its night spots.

I was up and on the road before sunrise and past Olympic Stadium before the first surge of early morning commuters took to the road. It was mid summer and I was at least two weeks ahead of the game. I was now entering rural Quebec. Fields were pregnant with crops and a warm breeze blew off Lac Saint Pierre mixing with the rich smells of pastoral farmland. Church spires now marked the entrance of every village and roadside crucifixes became so much confetti.

The land surrounding the Saint Lawrence was rising. Farmland began to look like so many strip bowling alleys dropping down to its waters, but it wasn't until I had passed Baie Saint Paul, east of Quebec City and climbed up the near vertical 1:20 gradients of Route 362 that I saw for the first time the vast ocean arm of the Saint Lawrence. I had been travelling so slowly from Montreal that this prolonged day in, day out association only registered as a channel. For a fleeting moment, it took my breath away. Ships now passed below me like slow-moving islands, power boats like ants, and I could even make out a pod of whales. 24 kilometers shore to shore it was almost as wide as the English Channel. I could see clearly the flat banks of the southern shore, its many villages and towns and the natural boundary of smooth hills I would have to cross to get into New Brunswick. So far it was the most impressive view I'd experienced since leaving British Columbia. I decided to camp that night on a bluff overlooking the river. The sun set into a bronze sky, and except for the occasional dull throb of pass-ing container ships far below, I was enveloped in silence.

The next day I found myself pondering over a minor decision at a shore line cafe in La Malbaie when a middle-aged couple joined me. I was heading towards Saint Simeon en route to the ferry trip across the Saint Lawrence to Riviere-du-Loup. The noon ferry was out of the question, and the scheduled mid after-noon departure would be touch and go, but the early evening ferry wouldn't arrive at the south shore of the Saint Lawrence until after dark. That would mean a night spent in a hotel and hotels in Riviere-du-loup, I had been told, were very expensive.

"Bonjour, Mr. Howgate."

Mr. Howgate, good God. They knew my name. Apparently my fifteen seconds of fame had followed me from Montreal. We exchanged the usual pleas-antries, the why's and wherefores, then got down to the nitty grittys of life.

If I ever thought my chosen life was odd, then meeting this couple sure put it into perspective. Denis turned out to be an ex-priest and Claire, his wife,an ex-nun. They had met on a retreat, became friends first, later lovers, then shortly afterwards - having left the Catholic Church - partners in life. They had re-entered the real world in their mid forties, but due to their cloistered world, life hadn't yet smoothed down the rough edge of their naivete. They introduced me to the history of the region which before the three towns of Trois-Riviere, Baie-Comeau and Sept-Iles were developed, had supported people whose living on the

North Shore came from the scenery, fish, clams, forest and agriculture. Then, inevitably, they turned the conversation to church matters.

"Have you noticed the lack of youth?" Denis asked. "It was only a generation ago that the church dictated all aspects of family life in this region and that meant the population. Have you heared the term Vatican Roulette? That's what they call the rhythm method in Quebec. Now it's the pill and the abortion clinic." He was a breath of fresh air and kept up a lively conversation, dotting the I's and crossing the t's of many a silent question. As luck would have it, they were going in my direction. They were on their way to Fredericton and left with a promise to meet later at the ferry terminal. "Don't worry about a place to stay Bernie. I know the priest in Riviere-du-Loup."

Now I could relax. I could enjoy the views and freewheel to my hearts content. I had spent two weeks in Quebec and only one night under the stars, and that was by choice. I had spent the first night in Lachute when a garden barbecue had stretched into a night between clean sheets; Montreal with old friends and, in Trois-Rivieres, I was seduced by the thought of mixed dorm accommodation at its youth hostel. At Donnacona, I had been waved down by a group of wedding day revellers only to find myself emptying too many glasses of wine and passing out on some collective couch. In Sainte Anne-de-Beaupre it was a millionaire's designer-built home, star gazing under its cathedral loft-glazed roof, and tonight promised to be yet another kind of indoor surprise.

Denis met me as promised in Riviere-du-Loup, acted as translator, then left me in the capable hands of Father Jacques. I didn't, as I had thought, end up at the steps of the church or gain entry to the priest's house. Instead I was given, free of charge, a room set aside for visiting church guests at a local motel.

Chapter 14
Humour and Unemployment

For three hours, I climbed into the foothills of the Gaspe Peninsula. The hunchbacks and switchbacks of the north shore had smoothed on its southern bank. Forest had overtaken farmland and ski economy that of rural. It was one of those days when you knew miles would be covered, but nothing else. Six miles before Edmundston, I crossed the border into New Brunswick and officially entered the Maritimes and yet another time zone.

The Maritimes have two main ingredients that set them apart from the rest of Canada, humour and unemployment. I had been told that Boston had more Newfies working there than St. John's and that during Maine's berry picking season, Maritimers had been known to rise from the dead, go south and take on its seasonal work.

New Brunswick, as any student of geography knows, is the last province on mainland Canada as Prince Edward Island and Newfoundland separated shortly after a heat wave in the Ice Age, and Nova Scotia likes to think it's separate, as that piece of chewing gum that sticks it to the mainland is likely to snap any day.

From Edmundston, the Trans Canada Highway followed the graceful curves of the St. John River. I was now cycling over relaxing hills, smooth turns and long drawn out straights. On the south side of the river the 'Stars and Stripes' were a constant reminder of Big

Brother's presence, and their larger houses of their greater wealth. I was cycling through a rich corridor of farmland interrupted from time to time by old world 'white' wood villages centred by enormous stone churches. The river seemed to follow the pattern of its inhabitants, unhurried, broad, and graceful. I called in a shop and had to wait until the local gossip had been spelled out. It was obvious that the ambitious had either long since departed for the richer pastures of Ontario and Alberta or been swallowed by the tides of the Bay of Fundy. New Brunswick is not for your urbanites. It has many more densely populated rural areas, as I was learning quickly. I had been taught in school that its main industry was the tree. All they had to do was watch them grow and cut them down, but one thing they had been able to raise besides forests, is rich men.

Take Max Akeman who went to England and sold newspapers until he became Lord Beaverbrook. Then came Jim Dunn McCain of potato chip fame and lastly, Casey Irving of Irving gas station fame. He's the fella that reinvented the game Monopoly and he's now resting in a tax-free haven called the Bahamas. It's a province of extremes, and stopping for the night in Woodstock, I was introduced to yet another form of employment. The underground variety.

"What are you goggling at?"

There aren't many experiences more embarrassing than being caught in the act of voyeurism. For twenty minutes, I had been riveted in curiosity, watching the young man across the street, as first one person then another stopped in their cars to talk to him. I had twisted and curled my imagination around the suitcase he opened during each encounter. What was inside? He had looked out of place from the word go. Long, jet black, beaded hair, heavy build with a smart royal blue jacket, white dress shirt, jogging slacks and runners. He looked a cross between a smart businessman and a child of reggae. He just sat on the pavement bench wearing an expressionless look of boredom, like a young boy trying his best to ignore his surroundings. Then, for no apparent reason, he crossed the street towards me.

"Got a problem?"

He had a real look of menace in his eyes.

"Think ya' better than me do ya'?"

I was just forming a reply when he dropped his suitcase on my lap.

"Open it."

From the look on his face he wasn't going to take no for an answer and his size only reinforced it.

"That's what I do for a living, so what ya' going to do about it?"

Inside, brand new, still with their custom seals, I counted at least thirty American 'Rothmans' cigarette cartons.

"Cop, eh?"

There was no give in his tone.He thought I was a plain clothes policeman and caught in the act, he wanted his show down.

"Why don't you pick on somebody else. We've all got to make a living, eh."

He was talking so fast, I couldn't get a word in edgeways. Then he saw the rickshaw, stopped in mid sentence and I jumped in.

"Ever seen a cop with one of those?" He turned

out to be not only a man big in stature with equally big gestures, able to order drinks all round with one tiny motion of his finger. His friends came and went like a revolving door, and soon our table was full of empty beer bottles. He seemed to know everyone by their first names; it was either that, or he was related to everyone in Woodstock. His stories would start out at Jack's bean stalk height and get taller with every telling. We stayed only the length of time to see his first round complete its circle and when no one else was willing to dip any further into their pockets, he left with me in tow.

"Come, you can stay at Doris's place. She'll have a meal ready at this time."

He wasn't exactly squeaky clean, but then I'm no saint either and after all, I owed him a round of drinks, and if he wanted his pound of flesh, so be it.

"Hello, Baby."

He strode into Doris's home like he owned it, then set about charming her till she was limp and putty in his hands. What the hell, he was an original. He just wanted an audience to watch his conquest, and today it was me. He looked equal parts devil and saint with piercing brown eyes and a swagger that only a good physique carried from childhood can give you. There was no grey matter in his character. The male came a poor second to this man and, except for the occasional wink in my direction, I wasn't even allowed the honour of a bit player to his dinner time conversation. He ate on the move, an animator's delight while holding a rapid fire conversation. You obviously got what you saw and Doris was impressed beyond words. In fact, I can't remember her saying more than two yeses and one no. Maybe it was the no. I can't remember when she said it, or to what end it was directed, but I do remember it altered the whole atmosphere and ten minutes later my friend left me to pick up where he left off with a nod and a wink and, "I'll see you tomorrow". I never did see him again and I never did get past first base with Doris. Once again, I ended up sleeping on a couch and woke the next morning to the pungent smell and delicious crackling of a bacon and egg breakfast.

In these parts the weather is as uncertain as a baby's bottom. Hot and balmy one moment, wet and damp the next, and today it had the added quality of a hot flush. It was hotter than hell in Keswick, humid and wet in Nashwaaksis and down right monsoon-like as I entered Fredericton.The rain got everywhere. It forced its way through layers of plastic bags to rinse my spare clothes, soaked my sleeping bag and turned my freshly donated American cigarettes into limp storks.

I turned up at Fredericton Youth Hostel like a sad-eyed seal, pleaded with its Youth Hostel guardian for a dry towel, then showered and fell into a much needed sleep. For once I could close the door on travel. I was in luck. I was the hostel's only paying guest, and for four uninterrupted hours, I was dead to the world. Sadly this peace didn't last long. On the second day three pimple faced students of revolution gate crashed my solitude. It's not that they stamped around the dormitory or that they decided on their beds to hold their round table discussions; it was when I heard the whispered name of my home town being dragged into the gutter.

I found early on that to mention I was from Toronto was to invite a storm of good-humoured abuse. On a scale of one to ten, it was right up there in the big leagues competing with sport and sex for importance. From Victoria to Montreal, even in its home province in northern Ontario, its name had sparked equal doses of vomit and praise. Canada's equivalent of the 'Big Apple', it had what dreams were made of. Money, sex and romance, and opinions on its worth fell into two camps. Those who loved it and those who hated it. There was no middle ground. Outside a few 'passers through', I hadn't spoken to anyone who had lived there. Information was always secondhand, larger than life and full of colourful anec- dotes. Most peoples' experience with T.O. starts and ends with the early evening news. If you are a pre- teen, it's Much Music, and if you are a member of the silver-haired set, it's the demon place that took their children away. I gave up after Calgary trying to correct their misinformation and by Winnipeg, I was down to nodding in agreement. In Montreal, I dodged the bul- let and became a new immigrant, but here in Fredericton, I felt compelled to re-enter the debate. It's not that I feel a strong affiliation towards T.O. I have been transplanted so many times in the last twenty five years, that it is hard for me to hang my hat on any one place. I feel just at home in Calcutta as I do in Toronto, and no more out of place in the small com- munityies in Labrador than I do in a sprawling metrop- olis. It's just that no one holds a gun to your head and forces you to live anywhere these days, and if you want to chase money you have to pay your dues, and if that means cutting the umbilical cord of family ties and selling your soul to your employer, that's your problem. I gave them both barrels and threw in my age just to irritate them. I couldn't ask for a better appetizer and by the time my mouth had run its course, I was ready to greet the day and eat whatever meal was put in front of me.

I found Fredericton's main street sleeping peacefully in the sun. Bells were chiming and their spires of religion were thrusting their tips above the city's majestict corridors of elm. I reveled in the laid back hospitality that only those through age, or untouched by the seduction of money, could offer. Almost everyone I passed greeted me. I was surprised how the arm of suburbia reached even down to the city's main street, where children played unworried by traffic and young and old alike jay-walked. Trees, some huge and as ancient as the houses they shaded, arched a hundred feet above the ground. Houses came straight out of Victoriana, fit for the landed and gentry. Residences for the prosperous with turrets, patios, secluded verandas and with exterior walls made in gingerbread fretwork surrounded by fortified gardens, allowing the kind of privacy that some Torontonians would mortgage their souls to own. Many were still family residences, but many more with new fire escapes and apartment vacancy signs had split to cater for a new class of occupant. I walked around Fredricton like one does a well manicured maze, enjoying the feeling of being lost, knowing I wasn't too far from home. In fact, everything I saw that day wasn't too far from home.

I stayed embraced in the warmth of Fredericton's easy-going lifestyle for six days. I ate and walked, but mostly slept the clock around. My dormitory companions only stayed long enough to catch the next bus out for Halifax and I owned the dormitory for a further three nights. I felt rejuvenated. My bike was in tip-top shape. I had replaced the old foil around my handlebar stem with new, oiled and greased all moving parts and exchanged my worn out plastic-covered seat with one made from sweat-absorbent leather.

I left Fredericton on the Trans Canada Highway en route to Moncton. The unseasonable early morning heat haze hadn't evaporated and a thick mist hung over the St. John River. For twenty kilometers the road zig zagged along its sleepy banks. The countryside was lush, green and flat, broken only by the occasional splash of colour called communities, too small to be called villages and too large to be called hamlets. They fell between the no man's land of community services and, with no convenient stores, were irritating to cycle through.

By mid morning the sky was bleach white and sun flashes burnt my skin like boiled water. The river was beginning to look more inviting by the minute and just past McGowan's Corner, I took the plunge.

I should have looked first, but once the germ of a cooling swim took root, my brain shut down and my body took over. I should have known better. It wasn't the cold that sent shivers down my spine, not even the green dust like fungi that covered my skin, it was that object that was floating towards me. At first my eyes wouldn't believe, even my nose doubted. But when the object closed-in and its shape took form, my body kicked into over drive. Not a dozen feet away, bloated, half submerged and rocking in the current, but still recognizable, was a dead dog.

I was glad to put the morning behind me. At Young's Cove, I turned north on Route 112 and followed the Canaan River's course into the rugged farmland of Westmorland County. Once again I could relax. The road was deserted and what breezes there were only added to my feelings of peace. That night I could have chosen a million-and-one camp sites. The sky was clear. The river bank open and dry, and just about every field owned a shelter of trees. Once again, I was seduced indoors by an open-ended invitation. A casual conversation roadside 'drop in for a cuppa tea when you get to New Cannan' and before I could change my mind, I was seated amongst an army of children with a feast of fresh farm produce fit for a king.

In Moncton, I made the decision to take in Prince Edward Island. If I was going to say I had cycled across Canada, then I should also be able to say I had cycled through all its provinces. There was one more compelling reason. A link bridge connecting PEI to the mainland was in the works. The start date was still five years in the future, but then I might not be this way again and I didn't want to miss the opportunity to ride its ferry service.

I left the Trans Canada Highway and turned east on Route 134 and the more scenic road to Cape Tormentine. I was doing fine. I had started the day with a large farmer's breakfast of freshly-made bread, garden jams and a huge steak of bacon. In Moncton I had called in the main post office, picked up my mail and then spent hours reading and rereading their contents. The heat wave was history, and a late August chill had condensed the humidity. I should have been on top of the world, but a bubble in my stomach burst near Shediac and within minutes,I was racked with cramps.

I'm not one for medicines. I haven't taken an aspirin since I was a child. I have lived out doors for years and have found the natural sweat of physical exercise my medicine of life. I don't need alcohol to drop my guard or drugs to give me a high and, no matter how worried or discouraged I get during the day, a night under the stars cocooned in the warm glow of an open fire is the only tonic my body and my mind crave.

There are few things more therapeutic, or more medically reliable remedies to mend one's body and soul than a good old-fashioned camp fire. I love everything about them. The wood collection, their lighting, their sound, their smell, and especially their warmth. No matter how weary and discouraged or sick I got during the day, the thought of a fire gave me an indescribable lift. I am one of those borderline pyromaniacs who could never put a matchbox down until it was empty. I look forward to these periods of fire building, especially my first hot mug of tea. For me, coming from England, the partaking of tea is something akin to a religious experience. Just consider a blazing fire, the humid hiss of boiling water and the background whistle of wind through leaves. I have always been an addict, but tea stewed in a smoke-stained pot, balanced on a twig over an open fire, sugar by the spoonful and drunk while sitting on a carpet of sweet-smelling balsam boughs, is the best tea of all. I'd learned my camping and fire building technique by trial and error; to camp close to slow moving water; to be far enough away from the road that its sight and sounds were muffled, and to be close to an ample supply of fire-bordering rocks. Wood was never a problem and, lately, neither were the mosquitoes.

It was now after dark and the half moon had turned the countryside into a lunar landscape of pale white. I slept without the protective cover of my mosquito net. The fire was dying. Flames extinguished and fell inwards with a soft cindery sound and yellow sparks illuminated the surrounding spruce like amber strobe lights. My stomach had healed and was now lined with a fresh coating of peanut butter. The CBC shortwave crackled, wavered in and out, then skipped stations. One minute, I was listening to the weather forecast and the next to the soothing tones of Margo Timmins, lulling me to sleep. The fire had been a perfect centrepiece for all my thoughts, but its flame had long since died and, with it, its umbrella of security.

We all have hidden fears. They can be shared by loved ones, suppressed in crowds or blocked out through activity, but sometimes there's no escape. I've had my fair share of these temporary visits to insanity and no trip is complete without at least one visit to your soul. Loneliness is always the main ingredient. I have always been seduced by the far away place, the one that begs adventure. Fear of the unknown is natural, but throw in fatigue and then illness, and you have a cocktail as strong as rocket fuel. Fear can be real or imaginary. I have never suffered from the real variety. If I can touch, taste or see it, I can cope. If it's abstract, I can't. My fears are elusive. They can be triggered by music, a shape in the water, or a cloud in the sky. Tonight it started with a silhouette. A twisted tree. The crack of a branch and the jaws of hell opened to devour me. It was awful. My legs were like rods of heated lead and my sleeping bag engulfed me in a claustrophobic feeling of helplessness.

God knows how I got out, but I did. The snake-like shadows had unravelled themselves and returned to their branches. The stars again looked friendly and the cool night sobering. I relit the fire, brewed another cup of tea and settled back into my sleeping bag for a restless night. We all have our different ways of coping with low points. Some search for hidden meanings and others, like myself, try to laugh them off and move onto the next as slowly as possible.

I was finding it increasingly difficult to concentrate on the here and now. My legs were peddling towards Tormentine but my head was travelling a different route. I caught myself walking down Queen Street, eating at my favourite restaurant and talking to friends. This in itself wasn't a problem. I often daydream, it's just that today I found it far too easy to stay in that state. I still had two thousand kilometers to cycle. I needed to get my act together and the tranquil atmosphere of Prince Edward Island seduced me like a warm embrace.

Chapter 15
Five lazy days in Summer

Jesus! The last time I saw so many Cadillacs and oversized Buicks was on the television series 'Happy Days'. The ferry to Prince Edward Island was full of gas guzzlers and grey hair, and shiny tops were the vogue. Before long, their owners were queuing to have their pictures taken with my rickshaw. To kill time, but more to escape the retiree brigade with cameras, I checked out the main deck only to be accosted by Lucy Maud. She was everywhere; in the stores, hung, stuck and taped on walls, even a sign reading Land of Green Gables watched over you in the washrooms. I'm not a devotee of orphan Annie, but it was difficult to escape her influence.

I arrived on the island at the tail end of their tourist season. The roads were empty and peaceful, with just the right amount of rolling hills to make progress pleasant. Farms looked self-consciously well groomed, as if waiting for their photographs to be taken. There was not a crooked furrow, unclaimed swamp, not a blade of grass out of place, or ragged tree in sight. Every field looked pregnant, bursting at the seams with everything from seas of yellow sun-flowers to miles of potato patches, and all were picture perfect.

PEI was quickly becoming the tonic I needed. Life slipped into a lower gear, even the farm dog's bark was more a token gesture than a pre-emptive strike. I was only hours into my route from Borden to Charlottetown, but the improvement in my outlook was amazing. I could breathe again. Aches and pains miraculously disappeared. Once again meeting people wasn't an obstacle to round, but a pleasant encounter. I was beginning to wind down like a spring and, after five lazy days in Chalottetown's cosy little youth hostel, I was ready to leave.

My whistle stop visit had turned into a battery charger and with the additional 'honk your horn and wave at Bernie' CBC interview, my progress that morning to the Wood Island ferry was a continual punctuation mark of hospitable noises and excited hand motions.

That there was any room for doubt as to whether my rickshaw would carry me to St John's, Nfld. was not in question. I had faced the chance of total machine breakdown every day since my accident in Montreal but it hadn't happened. Now at Caribou, N.S., I had to make another route decision. Getting spares in Charlottetown had been a stroke of luck. A chance meeting, a phone call and an afternoon of elbow grease with a bike enthusiast, and the rickshaw was as good as new. I now felt confident that the rickshaw was good for another one thousand miles. Once off the ferry at Caribou, I had no worries about pointing my rickshaw towards Yarmouth and the long way round Nova Scotia's coastline to Halifax.

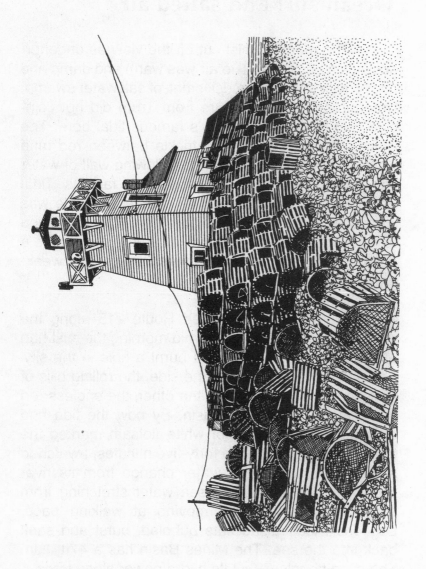

Chapter 16
Ocean surf and salted air

The morning mist cut off the view as ungenerously as a brick wall. The air was warm and damp and heavy with the sweet musk smell of salt water swamp. Unfortunately my departure from Truro did not coincide with the Bay of Fundy's famous tidal bore. The Salmon River was a mere trickle between red mud walls and that eighteen inch fast-flowing wall of water the tourist billboards advertised as its famous 'Tidal Bore' hadn't even reversed its course. The tide was still falling. Unless you were born here, I was told, you can never get used to the brown water tides. Twice a day on weekdays and three times a day on the weekends for the tourists.

From Truro, I followed Route 215 along the shores of Cobequid Bay. By mid morning the mist had evaporated and the sun had burnt a hole in the sky. The scene was weird. On one side, the rolling hills of lush green pasture and, on the other, the endless red mud flats of the Minas Basin. By now the tide had changed. A semi-circle of white flotsam marked the tide's speedy rise. Within forty-five minutes, I watched a mere basin artery of water change from its river width into a huge arm of sea water stretching from shore to shore. It was moving at walking pace. Lagoons filled, raised flats bubbled, burst and sank back into the sea. The Minas Basin has a 47ft, tide. The mind boggles. Just its hydro power alone trans

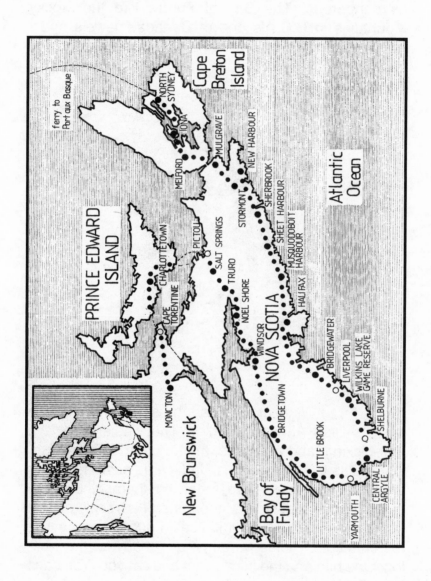

lates into twenty Niagara Falls and its traverse is just as dangerous. The Bay of Fundy, like the Rocky Mountains in B.C., is one of Canada's jewels and I wasn't disappointed that morning by the sight of its fast-flowing tidal waters.

   From Windsor, I started the slow climb into the orchard-filled Annapolis valley. The whole area is a fruit-picking and roadside market garden paradise. Carrots as thick as your fist, lettuce as crisp as crackers, and tomatoes were meals in themselves. You name it, they grew it, and the taste of a freshly picked apple was worth a detour in itself. I had timed my visit to perfection. Apples were ripe and ready for the picking. One bite and the juices spat back at you. You can't beat fresh fruit and, by day's end, I had a bag full of apples, a freshly made cherry pie bought roadside and enough donated tomatoes to keep me going until Halifax.

On sunny days you can fast forward daily frustrations, relax aching muscles and looked forward to healthy sun tans, but today the only thing I look forward to was finishing it. The sky went unnoticed and bends in the road, so much looked forward to on normal days - like the start of a new chapter - now piled one on top of another like so much unread mail. I was approaching Yarmouth, Nova Scotia's most southerly point. Peninsulas have always had this depressing effect on me. Getting there is no problem, it's the long haul back that kills me. I was only a day's cycling distance away from Yarmouth, yet already Halifax was weighing heavily on my mind. At Greywood, I could have shaved five days off my trip, but I didn't, and this morning's long range weather forecast with its depressing catalogue of lows, rains and falling temperatures only added to my mood, but by evening they were gone.

When all else fails on my trip, I fall back on my bread and butter pit stops. Baseball games not only act as end of day entertainment, but from under their players' dug-out, they offer the protection against rain and the curtain against the elements. There's something quintessentially North American about rounding bases, sliding over home plate and the crack of wood 'on leather. It's mother's apple pie and chewing gum all rolled into one. It's like watching grass grow while listening to cat calls. 'Have an eye. Take a ball. It's outa here'. I've never felt intimidated by either its spectators or by the manner in which the game is played.

Just as football and hockey have spawned their own breed of groupies, so has baseball. It's fundamentally a family-oriented sport. You don't have to purchase dollars of equipment to participate, be an athlete, or be a professor of statistics to understand that you have to round four bases to score.It's simplicity itself, although its television commentators would like to tell you otherwise. The game and the spectator go hand-in-hand, and it's this closeness that draws me to camp in their diamonds.

I stopped cycling at 7:00pm, was introduced to both sets of spectators by 7:30pm and had topped up my tanks with their gratitude by games end at 9:00pm. At 9:25pm the lights had gone out. The night sky reclaimed the stands and I slept where the players had been seated thirty minutes before.

The clouds broke early before breakfast and, by the time my wheels touched the road, the wind had changed direction and what clouds remained were soon lost to the horizon. I made Yarmouth in double quick time. I was under the influence of a strong tail wind and, as I rounded its peninsula and started on the return loop to Halifax, the wind changed to greet me.

For the first time since leaving Victoria, I had a 180 degree sea line horizon. It was fantastic. The fresh salt air pinched my nerves and its pungent smell ignited my senses like smelling salts. I now found myself cycling over narrow inlets, rising and falling into bays carpeted in lush healthy forests of fern, and crossing swollen rivers of sound. Within a morning, I had exchanged farmland for forest and agriculture for a fish-based economy, but sadly an economy that was on the decline, for about the only thing the eastern seaboard exports these days is its labour force.

For once, I was heading for a known destination. A friend of a friend in Alberta had passed on his mother's name and address with a 'Just tell me mum John sent ya and that I'll be home before Christmas'.

Just as it is true that for a person to truly understand the Maritimer one should see them in their own territory, so it is true that there are always two sides to a coin; those who stay and those who leave. John had chosen to enter the exciting lottery of those who leave and landed a twenty dollar/hour labouring job in Fort McMurray, Alberta, but the pull of one's roots is a strong one. To visit home in these parts means to visit your mother. Family ties are strong and where mother lives your home is, no matter how old you are. She expected nothing more and accepted nothing less. And when I arrived that evening with her son's name on my lips, I was immediately accepted like some extended family member. Short of a glazed eye at the mention of her son, I didn't even cause a hiccup in the old lady's routine.

Once I had passed Cape Sable, the eastern seaboard finally exposed its buttress of rock. The sea swells got noticeably bigger, and as the day drew on and the wind took off, it was soon a fury of pounding surf. Hills were getting steeper, switch backs narrower and more acute. I had started the morning following the rugged coastal 'Light House Route' with its stories of shipwrecks, rum runners and privateers. It had promised and delivered impressive views of the Atlantic Ocean, picturesque villages, knuckles of naked rock and what the Maritimes were famous for, rain and fog. The rain came in abundance, then the fog would roll in, rise in the late morning heat, condense on the inland hills, and return as rain in the evening. It was a cycle that would follow my progress all day and by the time I reached Shelburne, I had thrown in the towel. I was so exhausted, I staggered into the first restaurant I saw like a drunken man. Hunger immediately took over. Food travelled the least distance between hand and mouth and all pretense of table manners went out of the window. Within seconds my plate was licked clean and a second soon followed.

After two weeks of southerly air streams the weather broke. Summer finally said goodbye and for the next three days an easterly wind carried with it cold winds and scattered showers. I had covered all the distance between Shelburne to Halifax on Highway 103, bypassing the historical town of Lunenburg, the scenic peninsula of Mahone Bay and Nova Scotia's most photographed light house at Peggy's Cove. I was not in a mood for sight-seeing and, by the time I reached Halifax, all I wanted was a hot shower and clean sheets.

'HEALTH WARNING'

The centre of disease control in Ottawa has determined that ownership of bicycles has been linked to saddle sores, numb hands, backache, stiff neck, knee strain, leg cramps, chain rash, dog bites, constipation, acne, manic-depression, morning sickness, leprosy, diaper rash, nymphomaniac tendencies and sterility.

What a welcome. This notice, pinned to the bulletin board in Halifax's International Youth Hostel, greeted my first morning in their communal kitchen. Halifax was to be just a stop over. A one-night stand. But I found it easy to linger and the notice read, like its guardians, with contagious humour. There were no set rules and much of the food was on a shared basis. I could lull about for days in the kitchen, exchange stories with Mexicans, Japanese, Germans, Scandanavians and a very free-spirited girl from 'Down Under'. Here the term 'Saturday night in town' still had meaning. Drinking houses were nose to tail and gangs of high-spirited youths roamed the streets like wolf packs in search of game. Entertainment was crude, but not rude, loud but not deafening. People were grounded in basic necessities and easily pleased. I had a hell of a time. I abused my body for four nights and enjoyed every minute of it, then came pay-back time. Down Under, the Aussie thoroughbred I was trying to court, thought I required a crash course in detoxification before leaving, and that meant a 'Health Club'.

I'm not exactly an armchair quarterback, but I don't qualify as a professional athlete either. When she first mentioned I should sweat it off, I thought she meant a mixed sauna. She talked of pecks, quads and cardio while for me health clubs just meant ass and tits. When she told me she'd booked us into an aerobics class and that all we needed were shorts, sweatshirt and runners, I thought any sport that required such a dress code would be no problem.

Holy shit! I was only five minutes into the step routine and already suffering from cardiac arrest. The plump lady on my left hadn't even broken a sweat and

'Down Under' was going at it on my right like there was no tomorrow. I bit the bullet, or was it my pride, for ten more minutes. The music had gone from reggae to punk and bodies were gyrating and flying around like some kind of Hare Krishna love dance. I didn't see one pained expression, or another body like myself bathed in sweat. I lasted until half time and while everyone was into stretches and admiring themselves in the mirrors, I made myself scarce and hit the sauna.

I don't know if I was overly trained or still numb from yesterday's pain, but I remember little of the next day's experience. I do remember crossing the bridge to Dartmouth, because my teeth never stopped chattering from the cold, but the rest of the day was a blur.

That night the moon found me on the banks of the Musquodoboit River. The air was thick with perfume and above the stars were dancing. A coyote howled, a raccoon came calling, followed by squirrels on one last forage before sleep hit. My fire was crackling with heat and my belly was heavy with the sweet taste of beans and molasses. A lone goose lost at night flew overhead crying and I went with it. I was far away. The river was only a murmur and I fell as I lay in my sleeping bag into a deep, deep, sleep.

Rat, at, at, at.... Rat, at, at, at.... Rat, at, at, at.... Last night I was so tired, I could have slept on nails. I needed sleep like a thirsty man needs water. I'd even told my alarm clock to take the morning off.

Rat, at, at, at....

Boy, does this bird like noise. Under normal circumstances, I would have enjoyed its presence, but to be rudely woken at dawn by a headbanging woodpecker beating hell out of my rickshaw's wood-framed seat was enough to drive me crazy. But the best was yet to come. Having opened my lids to the light, there wasn't a hope of closing them. I broke camp, walked down to the river, cleaned my teeth, sponged my face and just caught my reflection in a stilled pool of water when I saw it....

It was the kind of scene *National Geographic* open their vaults for. On the far bank, not thirty feet from where I stood, dwarfing the rock it rested on and tearing apart a salmon with the ease of a razor blade, was a golden eagle. It hardly gave me a second glance and, with the exception of one swiveled motion of the head and a momentary stare down, didn't even acknowledge my presence. I watched it for ten minutes. Blood oozed out where claws sunk into silver flesh and although the half-dead salmon kept up a continual effort to free itself, the eagle never even flinched.

When I crossed the bridge thirty minutes later, the eagle was still there. The salmon was now open from head to tail and the banks of the river lined with feathered spectators awaiting their turn. I was on cloud nine. An eagle. I couldn't wait to share the experience and by mid morning, I was bursting with its story.

Good God, what a hooter! I'd stopped at a variety store ready to stretch my eagle's beak into the story of a lifetime only to encounter in reality one of equal size. Not in my whole life had I seen one that big. It set out from its owner's bridge intending to be distinguished, even classical, then half way down it began to spread, flatten out and take on the curve of a sailboat's keel before turning in on itself. It was huge and, try as I may to keep eye contact, I just couldn't.

"Fine weather we are having."

I had forgotten what I had called in for.

"I'm just looking around. Haven't made up my mind yet."

Two beaks in one morning. I guess lightning can strike twice in the same place. I left with a packet of envelopes and a pad of writing paper. I took the safer route of penning the incident of the eagle to friends and leaving the other to a later date.

The road from Halifax to the Canso Causeway was the best yet. It was as if time stood still. My pace, like the people I met, became leisurely and relaxed. Villages scattered and stuck like limpets to rock. Bays opened, inlets closed and points of land were lost to thunderous surf. The people, like the land they lived in, were rugged, full of character and reflected its untamed beauty. For five glorious days, I ate at the table of east coast hospitality as invitations to spend the night followed every handshake. Sheet Harbour, Sherbrooke, Stormont, New Harbour, Mulgrave. From fisherman to vicar, I graced their tables, shared in their stories, downed their home brew and sang along with their impromptu choirs.They lit up my life and pulled at my heart strings. I ate moose, rabbit, crab, cod, salmon and every variation of wild berry pie you could think of. The smell of bread fresh from the oven stained the air of many a kitchen and I lost count of the cups of tea I downed and the number of times my bloated stomach and bladder visited the toilet . Had it

not been for the first hints of autumn colour and the
need to finish my trip before its cold, wet easterly
winds set in, I could have stayed much longer.

I arrived at the Canso Causeway just ahead of
a storm. The sky was getting blacker by the minute.
The air was wet, not with rain, but with something
between drizzle and mist. Clouds hung like suspend-
ed ceilings cutting out the tops of hills and smothering
Cape Breton's highland mountains beyond. It was
going to rain alright, maybe not now, maybe not in
sixty minutes, but it sure as hell was going to catch me
sometime. I was beginning to feel like a condemned
man and I wanted something warm to line my stomach
before it caught me.

When I arrived at the Causeway, it was like a
wind tunnel. I wasn't in a mood to be picky. I stopped
at the first truck-stop I came to, ordered breakfast and
sat down to an egg sandwich, or what loosely passed
as one. But in truth, truck stops give you what you pay
for. And price aside, one thing always remained constant, its coffee.Fresh day or night, and always strong.
One hit was good enough to straighten the most
rheumatic toe, pry open the sleepiest lid and was better than any electric shock treatment to put colour in
your cheeks. But what I needed that morning was a
shot of brandy.

The wind was now so strong it pinned my ears
back. The Canso Strait had been whipped into a fury
and its spray was airborne. A truck warning was in
effect and all high load vehicles were advised to cross
with caution. My canvas canopy was in tatters and so
were my nerves. One hour later, the shakes started.

Hypothermia was coming in waves. My hands were freezing and my cheeks red raw. My nose was still there, but its barometer had shut down. Then just before Glendale, I compounded the situation and took a wrong turn. Soon the paved road disintegrated into gravel, then a hole the size of a mine crater swallowed me. It took a return trip to the highway, a 50/50 judgement call and one hour later, I found my motel in Melford.

"Do you want the special?"

I was dying in front of her and all she wanted was my money. If the situation wasn't so laughable, I could have cracked up. Here I was bagged and ready for the freezer. My fingers were white and lifeless and I was still wearing the garbage bags of protection over my shoulders and feet. I must have looked like something from 'outer limits', but she hadn't batted an eyelid. To make matters worse, the room she offered was like a block of ice, but a propane heater soon solved that problem and once I'd showered, slipped into bed with the TV remote, the world, for the first time that day, smiled on me.

The tourist information leaflet on my bedroom table said Cape Breton's interior was a rugged blend of mountains, valleys, rivers and lakes, but I would see none of them. A thick fog had descended that morning and squeezed out all my enthusiasm. I didn't want to leave the warmth of my bed, but you don't hold your breath in these parts waiting for the sun, because it could become terminal. The fog stayed for two days. I had planned to take the Cabot Trail. Take a short time out to go fishing and spend at least one Saturday night down at the Legion toe tapping to Gaelic music, but alas, it wasn't to be. I took the short cut through Iona, crossed its straights to Grand Narrows, then the long haul to North Sydney.

North Sydney is Marine Atlantic, and Marine Atlantic is the ferry service to Port aux Basques and Argentia in Newfoundland. I was so depressed, I could have caught the Argentia ferry and saved myself 1000 km in distance and three weeks in time, but I just missed the day's scheduled crossing and was too impatient to cross the Cabot Straits to Newfoundland to wait until tomorrow. Twenty minutes after my arrival at the ferry terminal, I had a ticket to Port aux Basques and four hours after that, I was saying goodbye to the mainland and heading for the 'ROCK'.

Chapter 17
The Rock

It is ironic that Newfoundland at forty-three years old is still the new kid on the block. The last province to enter O' Canada, yet the first to be settled on this side of the Atlantic.

"I lad, wan'a drink, does tha'?"

His words were original and sentences simple with a dialect whose tones, once released, snapped back like rubber bands.

" 'Ere boy, take one. I got a six pack unda' table. And there's plenty more where that cum from".

His six-pack went in short order. Then his mates came and it was onto the serious business of getting pissed and telling tall stories, and the deeper we went into the night, the richer and more animated their words and gestures became. A word such as 'gi me' sounds precisely like the order it makes - ' give me, or else' and ' bang belly', the Newfoundland word for a particularly greasy kind of pancake, anticipates the explosive impact for the thing it stands for. And is there a lovelier or more suggestive word in any language than the Newfoundland ' merry begot', meaning child out of wedlock?

We steamed through the night. The beers kept coming and the stories kept growing. Here the only rule was that a good lie was better than a dull truth. Sometime during the night, I crashed out. I remember hearing the lounge TV blaring out some MTV movie and the 'purser' asking a rather amorous young cou

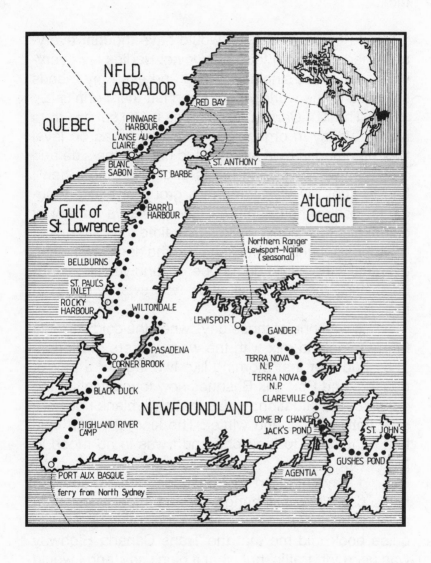

ple to take their copulating adventure outside onto the upper deck. But other than that, the six-pack did the trick.

In the morning you would have thought everybody had died from food poisoning. Bodies lay everywhere, couples, singles, groups and even my friends sat dead to the world where I had left them drinking.

The *MV Caribou* docked, as it had set sail from North Sydney in organized confusion. I was on level two, hemmed in by a steel-plated hull on one side and a sixteen-wheeler firing up its engine on the other. I had to fight my way through a group of excited students, dodge their cameras, and deflect a battery of onlooker's questions, while all the time trying to unknit the ropes securing my rickshaw to the deck. And when eventually the cargo doors opened and vehicles started to exit, the whole situation was swallowed-up in fog.

It was one of those days when the cold currents from Greenland mix with the warm waters of Florida. They had met that morning like two legs of a pair of trousers and Port aux Basques now found itself in the crutch of the situation. It was that chill, blank nowhere time between fall and winter. The kind of damp cold that penetrates to the bone and I was in no mood to take to the road.

I stayed in Port aux Basques for what seemed half a day. I was still hung over and it took more than a couple of coffees to comb back the cobwebs. My old guide book told me that the Trans Canada Highway was used for traffic, but what it didn't say, and I would find out before sunset, is that it is also dubbed as an open-air abattoir. It was the start of moose hunting season. I could hear the occasional crack of rifle fire and the muffled sound of their owners' ATVs. in the hillsides searching for their prizes. Before I'd rounded Table Mountain, I had already been passed by half a dozen pick-up trucks supporting antlers and cycled through two roadside pools of blood.

That afternoon went at a snail's pace. I was caught in a wind tunnel. Great gusts swept down from the Anguille Mountains, bounced off their big brothers' in the Long Range and probed my weak spots. It was shake, rattle, and roll time.I was freezing and no sooner had I made Codroy Pond, downed my first stiff drink at its roadside bar, than I was cuddled up in an abandoned garage, wrapped in an alcoholic glow.

What a difference a night makes. I woke to find a light breeze coming up the Gulf of Saint Lawrence. The fog had disappeared, the temperature had soared and Newfoundland had turned greener than green. It was as if the clock had been turned back and summer was being given one last crack of the whip.

Once past the Port au Port Peninsula, valleys broadened and the road now cut a straight path into a blurred horizon of spruce trees. The road would rise over one hunchback hill after the next in snake-like curves, and I spent the best part of the day getting off and on the bike, pushing, pedalling and freewheeling with only hilltop horizons to look at.

Newfoundland isn't exactly Bangladesh when it comes to population density and its highways aren't the 401, but I was never alone for long. All I had to do was acknowledge passing vehicles and I was assured of a conversation. Road users have a language all of their own, and as speech is to the pedestrian, so the horn is to the drive. After five months on the road, I knew all its subtleties.

The Short Horn. The excuse me type. Meant, 'you're entering my space'.

The Short Blast. The type that shouts out to be heard. Meant, 'you're bugging me',

And the Lean-on approach, 'get off the road or else'. For the novice cyclist it's advisable to keep abreast of these signals. A wave of acknowledgement can go a long way and, like dialects, will be answered differently from province to province.

In British Columbia, drivers use the slow west coast arc, commonly called the 'laid-back wave', while in Alberta, a cap tip commonly called 'the cowboy salute' is in vogue. Saskatchewan and Manitoba greeted me with 'high fives' and in Northern Ontario it was the 'military salute'. Forget Quebec, they drive too fast anyway, but watch out in the Maritimes. Their 'rolling head' technique can leave you seasick. And on the Rock, its abundant hospitality is also its major drawback, so keep your eyes on the road unless you want to spend the whole day in conversation.

On the open road, rules and regulations aren't worth the paper they're written on, and what enforcement there is can't be seen beyond city limits. Between cities the rule of thumb is 'the biggest rules'. Everything, and I mean everything, gets out of the way of trucks. Cars give way to buses and bicycles give way to all the aforementioned. And if you're unlucky enough to be a pedestrian, you're worth five points. A moose, by the way, is worth three except here in Newfoundland where damaged goods are worthless.

Travel chooses me, more than I choose it, so it came as no surprise when at the junction of 430 and the TCH in Deer Lake that I took its northerly arm with only the idea of going to Labrador. Once again the seductive pull of a remote area had touched a nerve. The end of my trip was just around the corner in St John's, but I wasn't ready yet to greet it. My bike was in good working order and I felt fitter than I had in years. There had been a hint of frost in the morning dew, but the midday sun still held the power of heat. The days were getting shorter and the nights longer, but the thought of adding another flag to my impressive list of provincial flags attached to the back of my rickshaw stroked my ego.

God, my back was killing me. Not since Kicking Horse pass in B.C. had I felt the sharp knife edge of pain in my spine. I'd left Deer Lake thinking I would make Willowdale by mid afternoon. It was now early evening. My shoulder harness bit into my skin, furrowed my shoulders, and closed down my blood vessels. I was bathed in sweat and every time the sun's rays lost themselves to a cloud, my whole body shivered. I was on automatic pilot, bent double and wishing I was in another place. Gros Morne mountain was still hidden to its foot hills and each bend I turned and each road crest I summited, I prayed I would see it. And as if to make matters worse, the wind had played a cruel trick. I had started the 430 with a tail wind, but no sooner had I started the long pull up Gros Morne's gradients, than it had swung 180 degrees and was now acting like a mill stone around my neck.

My body had already started to shut down by the time I reached Willowdale, and the only signs of life that Saturday evening my eyes could latch onto was its only variety-cum-gas bar. The sun had already dipped below the surrounding hills and my mind was already suffering from the first signs of panic.

"Do you know if I can camp down in the church tonight?" I was grasping at straws. In these remote locations, variety stores dub as post office, library and the local internet of gossip. I was hoping the owner's network of contacts would come up trumps. My funds were low. I didn't want to pay out any money for a motel room and I didn't feel up to being public property in someone's house. I was completely exhausted and the church seemed my only choice.

"The vicar lives in Deer Lake, boy. I could give Clara a ring. She cleans up t' church. Maybe she's got keys."

Thank God it was Sunday tomorrow. We found Clara in the church and she not only lit up my life by giving me permission to stay, but also my belly by insisting I have a full meal at her house before bedding down for the night.

"What, you've never had a bake-apple cheese cake? Well you haven't lived until you have tasted one of mine".

I was sitting down in Clara's kitchen, and as her pie landed on the table my mouth dropped open. Her words had found a receptive vessel. I had just spent four hours bent double, fighting steep gradients and gale force winds. Now this lady was offering a taste of heaven.

A bake apple resembles in form a raspberry, has the colour of fresh salmon and in these parts are sought after like liquid gold. And if Newfies were given the choice, so Clara said, they would gladly adopt them as local currency. Bake apples are not so much a unique taste as a journey. I had bought and eaten some roadside in Corner Brook when I met some young boys selling them by the barrel -full. It's the pip that catches between the teeth that makes them special. And the combination of bitter and sweet sent my taste buds crazy but, I had never eaten them cooked.

They arrived on my plate and no sooner had she put a fork in my hand than the first mouthful went down the hatch. I'd never been one to turn food down and judging by the continual stream of cheese cake sections coming my way, Clara's cooking would test my storage capacities to the limit. Never short of words, I can be as silent as a lamb when eating and judging by my first bite, she'd lost a conversationalist but gained a fan.

From Willowdale the road stepped up into Gros Morne National Park, lipped over a crest and there to the north, barely visible through the fine mist and topped with a fresh dusting of snow, was Gros Morne. The view of the mountain was eerie. A surrealistic silhouette of silver and black. I had stopped and was just focusing my camera on its peak. I was trying to get some depth of field. A nearby tree and an overhanging branch, then suddenly my picture moved. An uprooted stump sprung to life. Twisted roots moved into a monstrous black shape with pointed horns. Under normal circumstances, I would have trained my camera on the magnificent beast, but moose were on the rut and you don't face down 500 lbs of brainless hormones unless you have a death wish or are just plain crazy.

"Arrr....Arrr....Ar.Ar"
"Arrr....Arrr....Ar.Ar".
I couldn't help it. You have to be a bit crazy to do what I do and any way, I was on a downward gra-

dient of escape. I tried my moose call again.

"Arrr....Arrr....Ar.Ar"

"Arrr....Arrr....Ar.Ar"

It stopped dead in its tracks. It was like show down at the OK Corral with one exception. I had no gun. The odds were weighted heavily in the moose's favour, but when you're hormonally driven, you don't exactly see straight.

Arrrrr.......Ar.

We were talking. It was amazing. My call worked. We stood staring at each other. Me rooted in excitement and my friend, snout in the air, trying to work out my body odour. I imagined the question he would ask me if he could, 'What's that?' There wasn't much difference between his surprised look at my rickshaw and the surprise that greeted it on a daily basis. What I took for granted, most people could only dream about. They couldn't even wrap their minds around the distances I had travelled, let alone the rickshaw's single speed, its weight and its psychedelic colours. When you start to think you can tele-communicate to animals, it's time to pack it in or see a psychiatrist. Outlined against the fine mist, the moose's hanging back looked huge. I could see its mane bristle and its flashing white flanks and massive forequarters quiver with nerves. We now stood staring at each other, more out of fright than curiosity. Then with a high kick, he turned. First a half step, then high stepping, not fast but regular with unchanging speed and with total disregard for any obstacle in his path and, as he took off at a gallop, I followed him. I watched him ascend a steep bank, then cut through some bush before disappearing behind a thick blanket of trees. Wow...!

I made Rocky Harbour by lunch time, then latched onto the horizon ahead for the long ride to St. Barbe and my crossing to Labrador.

I was now entering an open causeway boarded by sea and rock and by late afternoon I'd reached St-Pauls Inlet. The rain had stopped long ago. The sky was now open and blue and the seas in the Strait of Belle Isle were at rest with only a slow motion swell to distort its mirrored surface. The view of the road ahead was breathtaking. The peninsula's backbone rose like a great tidal wave through a purple haze. Bald hills rose almost perpendicular, while foot hills - for the most part wooded - rippled, then retreated more gently to rocky shores of shaved bluffs and salted inlets. Just before St. Pauls, the mountain range opened with seductive ease. A huge crack split the range in two and dropped into a shadowy chasm. Without a doubt, my trip had saved its best views till the last, but instead of being elated by the prospect of exploration, I was feeling an increasing emptiness and the knot in my stomach had tightened its grip. That night, I made camp adjacent to a creek with a view of the sea and an ample supply of driftwood. After making camp, I built a pyramid of fire. I watched it grow in size, then while its embers died, sat alone with my thoughts. Sleep that night was a luxury. I played out my trip over and over again in my head. I had returned from an eight year round-the-world bicycle trip in '88. I had gone two years without a fix. Two years without crossing over that invisible line. Was it now all worth it?

Being alone, I had told myself, was the ultimate

challenge. Like a boxer in the ring, there's no place to hide, no short cuts. I hadn't so much planned this trip as started it. I never knew from one day to the next where I would be sleeping. Luck didn't come into it. I had this blind faith in human nature and I fervently believed that whatever experience came my way, I had asked for it. You live down here, but your mind is up there. When does it all end? The moose sighting had shaken me up. One false move and I could have been just another accident statistic. Every mile was getting a little more important. Every day harder to get through. It's as if all these little side trips were putting off the inevitable. It was now becoming harder to finish than go forward, and that night I wept like a baby.

My trip went from bad to worse. For the next two days the weather closed in and the roads emptied. The Long Range mountains were lost to sheets of rain and the Northern Peninsula was beginning to look like a long black streak boarded by green with a yellow line down its belly. The spokes were coming off the wheels of my trip and my mind was spinning out of control. I was beginning to lose it. You can only revisit the trough of new experience for so long before it runs dry and the reality of life weighs you down. At Bellburns, I turned down an invitation to spend a night indoors for the seclusion of a fish shed. And in Barr'd Harbor, I chose an empty beach to be alone with my thoughts. I remember the moon's glow and the mountains rising like islands above the mist. I remember the sea's rhythm. The sounds of surf and the sounds of pebbles rubbing against each other. I can still picture my pyramid of fire, its sparks curling up in the heat and the occasional call of a far-off loon. The stars lit up the night sky like a million Christmas bulbs. It was one of those nights to be shared. The lone wolf returns to his mate, but my nest was empty. I'd hit rock bottom.

Chapter 18
God's Country

The ferry landed at Blanc Sabon, Quebec like an old lady would approach a railway crossing; precariously. Behind the town a bleak treeless wilderness greeted me. The ferry trip over from St Barbe had been rough. Frost was in the air and a strong north east wind had chopped up the Strait of Belle Isle and its cold damp air cut to the bone. The road to L'Anse-au-Clair, Labrador had been paved since my last visit in '80, but it was of little help. There were few trees to hide behind and even less shelter on the highland. Everywhere you looked was rock and the roadside peaty moss gave way under foot like crunched up styrofoam. I was already mummified in plastic bags against the wind and by the time I descended into L'Anse-au-Clair, I was iced.

"If you think its cold, here you should have been in Cartwright this morning, it snowed!"

Snowed! Christ what was I doing here? I had just pulled up at the village fish plant, struck up a conversation with a couple of locals and the last thing I wanted to hear was that winter had arrived in Labrador. It was now 9:00 pm. The houses were dark except for their window lights and I was desperate for shelter.

"Can I stay in the fish plant tonight?"

"You'll get no peace here, boy. Try, Jacques down the road. His store's still open".

The road back through the village looked even more pocketed and broken under the dull glare of street lamps than before. A thin film of ice crusted the puddles and above, the stars were dancing. I found Jacques' store at the end of the road and didn't so much meet the guy as have an audience. I had found him glued to the TV, but no sooner had his eyes latched onto me, when his mouth went into overdrive. This guy could make a sentence into a one-act play, and as for his jokes, they fell somewhere between the 200 word Ha Ha and the 5000 double Z. I let his mouth run its course, laughed in all the right places and spoke only when invited. Inevitably my rickshaw brought in custom and when one of his mates came into the store, and switched the channels of conversation onto my bike, I had the 'in' I was looking for.

At first, we fenced around the subject of a place to stay. He wanted yardsticks. 'What's the purpose of your trip? Why Labrador?' and the inevitable questions about haven't you got a girlfriend or children, both more directed at my virility that at any responsibility. He seemed to cover the A to Zs of life, but once he'd accepted my resume, the channels opened and we returned to the matter at hand.

"Sorry, but I don't know any place you can stay". He paused to watch my face, then laughed."Not many places around here is tha', but I know one if you don't mind rouhging it". He pointed to a derelict house over the road. "There's no lock on the door, help yourself". Then as an afterthought, he added. "Used to be my parents' place. They had seven kids". His eyes glazed over at the memory. "All gone now. I got one brother in Toronto and two in Halifax." By the time he'd gone through the whole family tree, he was in another world. He started to talk about the seal hunt, of days

when you could catch a barrel-full of cod from the village wharf and the boom days when everybody
worked. I could still recognize the hard edge of life in
his eyes, but once he returned to the present, it was
gone.

"If you want to use the toilet in the morning,
there's an outhouse at the back of me' shop. There's
candles in the kitchen and the water tap is in the base-
ment. Make yourself at home, nobody will bother ya'."
He turned off the lights, escorted me to the front door,
then left without a further word.

Housework dusting would have been like three
years hard labour, but I didn't care. The view outside
across the bay was spectacular. The full moon
streaked its surface like a silvery sash and flooded the
living room, filling it with shadows. The place hadn't
probably changed much since his parents were laid to
rest. On one wall, I could trace his family album and
on another, coated with thin films of dust but still recognizable, were pictures of past family boats. And that
night, I slept soundly on the living room couch surrounded by the history of Jacques' life.

I woke to a heavy frost.The living room window
had caught my breath and its patterns rainbowed its
edges. Yesterday's prediction of snow showers had
already arrived. Chocolate bars bought for just such
an occasion needed the old armpit treatment before
eating and my pre-packed sandwiches were as crisp
as chips. An Arctic high had collided with a low pressure system from Maine, and Labrador was getting an
early taste of winter.

Life is not always a Walt Disney picture. It's

hard to enjoy the scenery when the windchill is minus 10 degrees C and your lungs are bursting. To say it was a raw morning was an understatement. Cold, I am told, is just a matter of comparison while discomfort is just proof of one's bad adaptability. Those words were of little comfort. I was on a roller coaster of steep inclines, wind-swept barrens and freewheeling gradients to hell. Forteau, L'Anse-au-Loup and Capstan Island, each settlement was buttressed by huge slabs of rock that dropped like knuckles into the sea. My body was going from hot to cold, from sweat to chill and by mid afternoon, I had thrown in the towel.

Pinware River was no different in size or location than hundreds of similar settlements I had passed through, but once I had made up my mind to stay in one, whether by time constraints, night fall or, like today, an impending storm, it made them special. I felt that all eyes were on me, like an entrance on stage. It wasn't ego or conceit, it was worry. Would I find a place for the night? Had my name been passed down the road? Would people be receptive? I had spent thirty minutes doing the usual rounds; the variety store; the church, the local game warden. It was like an adrenalin rush, the closer to night fall, the richer its rewards, and today was no different. It was already twilight. The sun had set into a dirty sky. I was down by the fish plant. A friend of a friend of a friend had pointed me in the direction of a fishing boat called Jason and Jamie and the rest was history.

It was like we had been long lost brothers. Roger Flowers, his cousin and his boat. I was introduced to all three and as the two former left with a 'help yourself to all you find', I immediately settled back into a cosy bunk and fell asleep.

If you have never spent an evening on water you're missing a special treat. But to be offered the freedom of a boat without the responsibility of sailing it is the finest treat of all. I spent two days stormbound on Roger's dragger and by the end of the first day, it had turned into the local drop-in centre and by the end of the second, every one that was someone in the village had come around for a share in the travelling man's story.

The weather finally broke on the third day. The Northern Ranger the coastal ferry that knitted together Labrador's coastal communities and my only worry, had been stormbound and would arrive in Red Bay en route to Lewis Port in two days time. I had no intention of missing it. The Northern Ranger takes 10 days on its round trip up the Labrador coast, and the thought of being snowbound for over a week if I missed it didn't exactly fill me with enthusiasm. Winter was just around the corner and all the impetus to leave Pinware River.

Eight hours later the road abruptly stopped in Red Bay. A long arm of the sea water had thrust its way in between a crack of land and had halted my progress. I had turned the corner. The Strait of Belle Isle was behind me. And the Atlantic now cut deep furrows into the land. Red Bay was the end of the road and would be my last side trip before the finish line.

It was late afternoon. The sky was grey and the shoreline sterile. It was washing day and each house had its own paper dragon of clothes blowing in the wind. The scene was one of tranquility, an overlapping experience that before day's end would start in the Baptist Church, take me into a kitchen filled with the aromas of cooked food and end where it started, at the foot of an altar in my sleeping bag.

Sometime after midnight, I took a stroll. A lone dog barked, then silence. A vacuum emptied the night sky and a still, jet black sheen filled the bay. My eyes rested on its harbour, then turned to its black box-like silhouettes, each topped by white smoke that curled up as quietly as mist. I walked for hours, recharging batteries. I wanted to clear my mind. My trip was on a low ebb. I had one lap to go and I wanted desperately to finish on an upswing.

Chapter 19
The Finish Line

The hills above the inlet were on fire with the flames of autumn. It was like the season had ignited overnight with colour. I was back on the Rock. The Northern Ranger had steamed for eighteen hours from Red Bay and now I felt sky-high. I had experienced a bronze sunset, the seven veils of the Northern Lights, and awoke to a blood red sunrise. Once again I was ready to greet the day and no sooner had we docked in Lewisporte, than I was back on the saddle and ped-alling.

Once again the scenery changed. Trees grew, bush thickened and my vision telescoped down open roads. It was as if I had put down a romantic novel full of rugged coastal beauty and picked up a business journal filled with mine sites, hard hats and neon lights. And this change wasn't just reflected in my new surroundings, but also in its place names. Corner Brook, Grand Falls and Gander. These names are for Newfoundland safe, but boring and almost certainly imposed upon them by mainlanders parachuted in for the sole purpose of making money for mainlanders. A quick look at the map shows that place names in gen-eral were almost always vivid, original and apt. The spontaneous invention spawned from within bar rooms or after a failed love affair. Take for instance Sally's Cove. I wonder what she did to deserve a place name. L'Anse-Amour, Maiden Arm, Paradise Sound, Tickle Harbour, Ho Ho Bay and Heart's Desire. None

of these names owe anything to tradition. These were
the creation of men ruled by emotion and with strong
ties to both the land and relationships. But not all place
names suggest life's brighter side. You only have to
see Deadman's Bay to read into Newfoundland's
darker passions as well as its grim humour. Wreck
Cove, Confusion Bay, Barren Island, Misery Point and
Wild Blight. No other place in the world has consis-
tently suggested this fundamental human emotion and
imprinted it on place names, and now in the interior,
everything looked bland, lifeless or new.

The scenery didn't pick up until Port Blanford
but by Clarenville it was downright spectacular. After
so many hours in the splintered light of heavy wood, to
see more than a glimpse of the sea was reassuring
and my first sight of the Northwest Arm acted like an
aspirin to my head. Familiar sights calmed me down.
Snug Harbour's brightly painted houses and the
inevitable white churches painted to within an inch of
their lives. They all had purpose and reason and made
my presence secure.
From Clarenville the road took to the high
ground. The light was full, unobstructed and stroked
land and sea alike, softening outlines, diffusing, overlapping and investing in objects, bringing colour totally into focus. The east coast with its sheltered sea
arms and hidden coves offered subtle views that the
rugged Northern Peninsula couldn't match. I was now
catching a glimpse of Newfoundland's fairy tale.
Bonavista's Peninsula looked magnificent in sunlight
and magical in the soft rising mist. Hills were comfort-
ably rounded and heavily wooded to their tips. Gone

were the stark, jagged and aloof cliffs of Labrador. It was a delicate balance of beauty and the beast. Where land and sea met and where today's romance could, with a strong northeasterly, be tomorrow's death call.

From Jack's Pond, the highway began its gradual rise onto the natural causeway linking the main body of Newfoundland with the Avalon Peninsula and, in doing so, swept aside nature's order and design. This is obviously a place where God rested on the seventh day, then forgot it. Rocks pile high, one on top of the other. Here you could find all the materials of life, like a building site on strike. Rivers choked, trickled and lost themselves. Ponds are left indiscriminately in valleys and some, like lost sheep, on hilltops. Trees were almost non-existent, twisted at best, stumped through lack of nutrition, and everywhere tundra carpeted what soil remained. The highway had been squeezed into a narrow neck of land and the wind now swept over it at gale force. Suddenly the road would drop, go between two boulders, parallel a pond, then rise sharply before repeating itself. The causeway was quickly turning into a lunar landscape, but what a landscape.

At one point the wind changed direction, or was it me? I received a tail wind to end all tail winds and I covered 15 kms in double-quick time. On the flat, I could hardly pedal fast enough. Cycling up hills became a breeze and down hills the buzz of a lifetime, and it wasn't until I reached Chapel Arm that I took a much needed break to stack up on juices and chocolate bars.

What an epitaph for good healthy living I would make. I have been told I smoke too much, drink too little and eat all the wrong foods, yet at forty years of age, I can still hold up my end with the best of them.I had bust a gut pulling the rickshaw over the Rockies and burnt like toast in the Prairies. Ontario's vampires had sucked me dry, while Quebec got me drunk. In the Maritimes, I had suffered rising damp and now I could smell the finish line. In seven months, I had suffered nothing more than a ten-hour fever. This either spoke volumes for the outdoor life, or proved that the anti-smoking, vegetarian lobbyists were wrong.

The sun was already setting when I pulled into Gushue's Pond. The provincial park was closed, but that made it better: I would have it all to myself. I followed the gravel road down to the water's edge. Pulled two picnic tables together, waterproofed the tops with plastic bags, then set about collecting wood. The night air was damp and cold. Winter was just around the corner and my blazing fire was a welcome relief. I laid out all my remaining food, two potatoes, half a cabbage, one carrot, one onion and what remained of my jar of pickled rabbit. I diced up the vegetables, filled the pan with water, added my last thimble full of salt, then cooked the whole shooting match.

On a scale of 1 to 10, the smell of food cooking, mixed with smoke over an open fire after a day in the saddle, ranks a 9. Barring accidents, this would be my last night and I wanted to make the most of it. After tonight there would be no more nights under the stars. No more fires to focus my thoughts, and no more nights drugged by the adrenalin drain of a hard day of cycling. The axe was about to fall, so I savoured these last moments of freedom down to the last morsel of food.

After supper, I went for a walk. To the east, a rising moon was being eclipsed by clouds and to the west over Gushue's Pond the cloudless sky was blanketed in stars. All through my supper the end kept creeping up. With little to no planning, I had started this trip halfway through, then played catch-up ever since. Episodes had overlapped, individual experiences blurred, but friendships were still fresh. In Vancouver, a friend of a friend put me up for a week. In Calgary, a family opened their doors, sight unseen, on four hours notice and, in Flin Flon I became an extended family member who had an open invitation to visit again. I had been befriended, adopted and treated like a long lost son at every turn and it would only get better. By the time I'd reached Saskatoon my grapevine of contacts were welcoming me into their lives without breaking stride, and in Winnipeg, I became a surrogate father to five children on one hour's notice. In both Ottawa and Montreal it had been a delight to hook up with old friends and in Fredericton, Charlottetown and Halifax, I had relaxed surrounded by fellow travellers in the cosy atmosphere of their youth hostels. Between cities, I had placed myself at the doorstep of hospitality and not been disappointed, and tomorrow it would all end in St. John's. Was I such a nice guy? People had told me that my rickshaw trip was unique, disarming and because I was pedalling, identifiable. I now had no money left and no contacts to depend on for a night's stay. Typically, I was going to finish my trip as it had

started, on a wing and a prayer.

My last day and I was nervous. Would I have an accident? Would my bike hold up? The last lap is always the hardest. It's easy to fall into a new experience but hard to climb out of it. I had started this trip in Victoria on Sunday, 29th April and today it was Friday, 12th October. I had spent 167 days in the saddle and, including side trips, I had covered over 5,000 miles. The rickshaw was shaky but not broken. The handlebar wobbled like a drunken man and two days ago one of my pedals broke, but I didn't care. I was in a world of my own. Today, I would accomplish a dream few people have the time or motivation to complete: Cycle Coast to Coast across Canada. The Trans Canada Highway had dominated my life from the word go. It is no different geographically or politically, from that of the Grand Trunk Road which unites the Indian sub continent or the Trans American Highway which connects North and South America. They all cover about the same distance. All were built to open up new worlds and unite old ones. They are, in parts, used as footpaths for pedestrians, corridors for live stock, cycle routes, playgrounds for children, and lastly, a traffic route for motor vehicles. Wars have been fought over them, babies born on them and if accidents are a means of keeping the population down, birth control as well.

In Calgary, a rather animated truckie had told me that the Trans Canada Highway was also dubbed the world's largest parking lot. 'A wonderful road', he said 'The lots in St John's are full of cars from B.C. It's like they drove there and figured it wasn't worth the effort to drive back'. The truth is, I only cycled over one sixth of the TCH, but still it dominated my trip. Sure it felt as bumpy as a washboard in places and as dangerous as a mine field in others, but all in all, I found its surface to be smooth, its shoulders hard, and its sometimes neck-twisting bends and back-breaking, hunchback hills just enough to keep me honest. It's a wonder it exists at all, and as I dropped down into St. John's, I was glad it had been built.

Newfie or Bust